ASIA'S SOCIAL ENTREPRENEURS

Social enterprises of all forms drive inclusive growth by creating social and economic networks, and a stable ecosystem, that enable societies to grow and prosper. This book presents a collection of ten case studies that demonstrate the important role played by social enterprises in driving inclusive growth in Asia's economies.

Unlike the traditional models, such as NGOs and charities, that are donor dependent for funding, a social enterprise is a hybrid business model that includes both social mission and revenue generation goals to ensure sustainability and self-reliance. The ten case studies in the book provide a ringside view of how social enterprises operate and evolve to create, sustain, and scale up their social impact. Readers will gain a practical understanding of how social entrepreneurs struggle to maintain a balance between their two seemingly contradictory goals of creating social value and generating economic returns. The book carries the readers on the journey of each of these ten social enterprises, offering unique and valuable insights into the motivations, tribulations, successes, and even failures of these organisations—critical for continued learning, contribution, and innovation in the domain.

The book is appropriate for all readers interested in the role social entrepreneurship plays in stimulating economic growth in Asia, including organisations, government, and universities, as well as individuals.

Howard Thomas is an emeritus professor of strategic management at Singapore Management University. He was the inaugural Ahmass Fakahany Professor of Global Leadership at Questrom School of Business, Boston University (2015–2020). He was a 'serial dean' in business schools on four continents. He is the current dean of the Fellows college of the British Academy of Management. He is a highly cited scholar and has published over 40 books and over 300 articles. He continues to serve the academic community through his roles and fellowships in organisations such as AoM, SMU, and EFMD.

Havovi Joshi is the Director, Centre for Management Practice at Singapore Management University. She is also the Editor-in-Chief of *Asian Management Insights* and has served as a chief collaborator and editor on several book projects. Havovi is a widely published award-winning case author.

ASIA'S SOCIAL ENTREPRENEURS

Do Well, Do Good . . . Do Sustainably

Edited by
Howard Thomas and
Havovi Joshi

Routledge
Taylor & Francis Group
LONDON AND NEW YORK

First published 2022
by Routledge
2 Park Square, Milton Park, Abingdon, Oxon OX14 4RN

and by Routledge
605 Third Avenue, New York, NY 10158

Routledge is an imprint of the Taylor & Francis Group, an informa business

British Library Cataloguing-in-Publication Data
A catalogue record for this book is available from the British Library

Library of Congress Cataloging-in-Publication Data
Names: Thomas, Howard, 1943– editor. | Joshi, Havovi, 1969– editor.
Title: Asia's social entrepreneurs : do well, do good... do sustainably / edited by Howard Thomas and Havovi Joshi.
Description: Abingdon, Oxon ; New York, NY : Routledge, 2022. | Includes bibliographical references and index.
Identifiers: LCCN 2021017036 (print) | LCCN 2021017037 (ebook)
Subjects: LCSH: Social entrepreneurship—Asia.
Classification: LCC HD60 .A86 2022 (print) | LCC HD60 (ebook) | DDC 338/.04095—dc23
LC record available at https://lccn.loc.gov/2021017036
LC ebook record available at https://lccn.loc.gov/2021017037

ISBN: 978-1-032-06729-2 (hbk)
ISBN: 978-1-032-06731-5 (pbk)
ISBN: 978-1-003-20358-2 (ebk)

DOI: 10.4324/9781003203582

Typeset in Joanna
by Apex CoVantage, LLC

CONTENTS

ABOUT THE CONTRIBUTORS

Lakshmi Appasamy is an analyst and writer servicing international market research agencies, corporate service providers, and tertiary educational institutions. Her research interests include women's issues, social enterprises, social and economic inclusion initiatives, and business regulatory regimes. Based in Singapore, she has worked with eminent business leaders and professors and has co-authored several case studies, book chapters, and white papers representing a broad range of management subjects. A case study that she co-authored won the prestigious European Foundation for Management Development (EFMD) Case Competition Award under the 'Inclusive Business Models' category in 2016. She holds a Bachelor of Arts in English literature and a Master of Business Administration from the University of Madras.

Dr. Sheetal Mittal is a senior case writer for the Centre for Management Practice at Singapore Management University, with more than 10 years of experience in teaching and academic research at business schools. Her research, which focuses on marketing and consumer behaviour, has been published in peer-reviewed journals, including *Journal of Retailing and Consumer Services*, *Journal of Indian Business Research*, and *International Journal of Indian Culture and Business Management*. Prior to transitioning to academia, Sheetal worked with Nestle and Egon Zehnder in the areas of marketing and research. After graduating as an engineer, she completed her Master's in business administration from Faculty of Management Studies, University of Delhi, specialising in marketing. Later she went on to earn her Ph.D. in consumer behaviour from IMI, New Delhi.

Lipika Bhattacharya is a senior case writer and assistant director with the Centre for Management Practice, Singapore Management University. Prior to her current role, she worked in the IT industry for 18 years as a regional application director and senior project manager in multinational organisations like IBM, NYSE, NCS Singapore, Keane Inc, and Tele Atlas. She has worked in many countries, including Belgium, France, Canada, the United States, and Singapore. She derives her passion in writing from her extensive project management experience and a keen interest in research topics related to digital transformation and technology. She has recently won the Outstanding Case Writer award from the Case Centre for 2020. Lipika holds a bachelor's degree in computer science engineering with the highest distinction from VBU, India, and a masters in information technology with distinction from Singapore Management University.

CW Chan is a senior case writer for the Centre for Management Practice at Singapore Management University. He studied in the United States, graduating from Emory University with a double degree in political science and economics before attaining an MBA from Singapore Management University. Having previously worked in finance, he is interested in financial technology and innovations that have emerged from the industry. He has worked with many professors and industry leaders on a wide variety of topics that range from the lack of financial inclusion for lower-income workers to the use of sophisticated trading strategies by high net worth individuals.

Jonathan Chang's background is a mix of entrepreneurship, education, and public policy. Jonathan has founded and co-founded several technology startups across sectors in Silicon Valley, Manhattan, Singapore, and Jakarta - two of his ventures were funded by Y-Combinator and 500Startups. He was the Executive Directors of NUS Entrepreneurship Centre, NUS Overseas Colleges, and SMU's Lien Centre for Social Innovation (in which he pioneered the university's accreditation as Asia's first Ashoka Changemaker Campus). He has advised the governments of Singapore, Indonesia, Cambodia, Canada, and New Zealand on various entrepreneurship, innovation, and education related initiatives. As a global speaker and media commentator, Jonathan has given lectures and talks across six continents and written articles for Channel NewsAsia. He received the coveted European Foundation for Management Development Case Writing Award for documenting an innovative social enterprise in Bali. His TEDx talk at Harvard about the importance of a mission-driven life was featured in 'Voice of America'. Jonathan is a graduate of UC Berkeley, Stanford, and Harvard.

Dr. Aurobindo Ghosh is the programme director for Citi Foundation-SMU program for Financial Literacy for Young Adults (FinLIT) and the Inclusive and Immersive Experiential Learning Programme (I2XL). As an assistant professor of finance at LKCSB, Dr Ghosh has written award-winning research, published papers in areas of financial economics, and edited a forthcoming volume on the global pandemic. He teaches widely, including business cases in financial inclusion and social entrepreneurship, particularly in the ASEAN region. Dr Ghosh considers educators social entrepreneurs, demonstrated in the I2XL programme that aims to create an experiential learning environment for students to apply business concepts to real-life challenges and the FinLIT program that empowers young adults to pursue financial freedom.

Thomas Lim is a case writer with the Centre for Management Practice at Singapore Management University. He has had considerable experience conducting desktop research spanning political, economic, social, educational, and other policy areas for the Australian High Commission and the Embassy of the Republic of Korea. He has also carried out media monitoring, news summary writing, media report collation, and content analysis report writing for various corporate clients, many of which are Singapore government agencies and public-listed companies. Early on in his career, he was a B2B news portal and trade news magazine editor and writer. He holds a Bachelor of Arts (honours) in English language from the National University of Singapore, and a Master of Science in knowledge management from Nanyang Technological University.

Dr. Sin Mei Cheah is a business writer at Singapore Management University. She researches and develops case teaching materials for undergraduate, postgraduate, and corporate executive classes. Her case studies cover a variety of management topics, including sustainability, digital transformation, data analytics, entrepreneurship, family business, operations management, and others. She has published peer-reviewed academic papers in subject areas such as AI/sustainability, communications, and information management. Prior to academia, she has extensive project management experience in the ICT industry, specialising in healthcare, e-government service delivery, and communications, as well as in the banking and manufacturing sectors. She received her Doctorate of Business Administration from the University of Canberra (Australia) and Bachelor of Science from the National University of Singapore.

Miguel Angel Soriano is a fintech leader and green finance expert with more than 15 years of experience in investment banking, business development, strategy consulting, and project management. Currently, he works at IFC (private arm of the World Bank Group) and leads the Upstream efforts for the financial sector in the East Asia & Pacific (EAP) region. Upstream is part of IFC's ambitious growth strategy to stimulate investment activity to address complex development challenges in emerging markets. Miguel focuses on the origination and management of innovative projects that create new markets to solve development gaps and ultimately catalyze private-sector investments. On the academic front, Miguel finished his PhD thesis on the evaluation of fintech startups in financial inclusion in 2017. He is an adjunct professor at Georgetown University and a visiting lecturer at Cambridge University where he teaches fintech to the MBA and Master of Science programs.

Howard Thomas is an emeritus professor of strategic management at Singapore Management University. He was the inaugural Ahmass Fakahany Professor of Global Leadership at Questrom School of Business, Boston University (2015–2020). He was a 'serial dean' in business schools on four continents. He is the current dean of the Fellows college of the British Academy of Management. He is a highly cited scholar and has published over 40 books and over 300 articles. He continues to serve the academic community through his roles and fellowships in organisations such as AoM, SMU, and EFMD.

Dr. Heli Wang is Janice Bellace Professor of Strategic Management and Dean of Postgraduate Research Programs at Singapore Management University. Her research, which focuses on the resource-based view of the firm, strategic human capital, stakeholder management, and corporate social responsibility, has been published in various management journals, including *Academy of Management Journal, Strategic Management Journal, Academy of Management Review, Organization Science,* and *Journal of Business Ethics.* She has served as associate editor of *Management and Organization Review, Academy of Management Journal,* and *Academy of Management Review.* She also teaches and writes cases on the subject of corporate social responsibility.

Adeline Natalia Lai Sue Yi is an executive director at Standard Chartered Private Bank, with more than 30 years' experience in the finance and banking sector across organisations such as Citibank, DBS, UBS, and HSBC. She has an executive masters in business administration from Singapore Management University and a Bachelor of Business degree, majoring in economics and finance, from Royal Melbourne Institute of Technology (RMIT).

ACKNOWLEDGEMENTS

This book would not have been possible without the support of several people. We offer our sincere thanks and gratitude to the following organisations and people.

At the outset, we appreciate the support of the senior management at Singapore Management University (SMU), particularly Lily Kong, Rajendra Srivastava, and Arnoud De Meyer. We would also like to extend our special thanks to the faculty authors and our colleagues at the Centre for Management Practice.

We also offer our appreciation to the MasterCard Center for Inclusive Growth, which supports a global network of research partners and scholars to work on cutting-edge research on inclusive growth. SMU was among the research partners of the MasterCard Center and funded a Social and Financial Inclusion Research Program that ran from 2015 to 2017, led by Professor Howard Thomas, who was also appointed the MasterCard Chair Professor of Social and Financial Inclusion. Several of the case studies showcased in this book were developed as part of the Research Program.

And last, but most important, to each of those first-rate social entrepreneurs featured herein, thank you for taking the time to share your story with us. We have much to learn from your journey.

Professor Howard Thomas
Dr Havovi Joshi
Singapore Management University

INTRODUCTION

Sheetal Mittal, Sin Mei Cheah, and Thomas Lim

The concept of social entrepreneurship emerged in the 1970s when Europe experienced an economic slowdown, and persistent high unemployment rates and socio-economic pressures led to collaborations between the public and non-profit sectors.[1] It further rose into prominence in the wake of the 2007–2009 global financial crisis that highlighted the pitfalls of a pure profit maximisation approach.[2] Ever since, social enterprises have been growing at an accelerated rate, particularly in the emerging and developing markets of Asia and Africa, which face an overwhelming number of development challenges. In 2017, there were more than 2.3 million social enterprises in Asia alone.[3]

Large parts of these regions suffer from a high degree of poverty and extreme income disparity, coupled with inadequate infrastructure and under-developed legal and banking sectors, where millions have little or no access to critical life-enhancing services such as electricity.[4] In addition, low education levels and traditional cultural practices perpetuate inequities through discrimination on grounds such as gender, race, ethnicity, religion,

DOI: 10.4324/9781003203582-1

sexual orientation, gender identity, or disability status—thereby giving rise to insurmountable social, cultural, and financial barriers for the marginalised groups, denying them the right to dignity, security, and the opportunity to lead a better life.[5]

While the traditional forms of social institutions, such as NGOs and charities, work hard towards alleviating these ills, they often struggle with sustainability and scalability challenges due to the unpredictability of donations/funding received. These highly donor-dependent models of poverty alleviation often tend to curtail organisations' freedom to operate as well.

In contrast, a social entrepreneur adopts a hybrid business model that includes both social mission and revenue generation goals to ensure sustainability and self-reliance. According to Muhammad Yunus, founder of Bangladesh's Grameen Bank,

> *"Social entrepreneurship" relates to a person. It describes an initiative of social consequences created by an entrepreneur with a social vision. This initiative may be a non-economic initiative, a charity initiative, or a business initiative with or without personal profit. Some social entrepreneurs house their projects within traditional nongovernmental organizations (NGOs), while others are involved in for-profit activities.*[6]

The core objective of a social enterprise is to drive inclusive growth by ensuring the fruits of an economy's growth are distributed equitably to all levels of society, especially those at the bottom of the pyramid (BoP), and can be defined as having the following three components:[7]

1. identifying a stable but inherently unjust equilibrium that causes the exclusion, marginalisation, or suffering of a segment of humanity that lacks the financial means or political clout to achieve any transformative benefit on its own;
2. identifying an opportunity in this unjust equilibrium; developing a social value proposition; and bringing to bear inspiration, creativity, direct action, courage, and fortitude, thereby challenging the stable state's hegemony;
3. forging a new, stable equilibrium that releases trapped potential or alleviates the suffering of the targeted group and, through imitation and the creation of a stable ecosystem around the new equilibrium, ensures a better future for the targeted group and even society at large.

A social enterprise thus aims to deliver on these elements by creating both social and economic value. As Seelos and Mair say, a social enterprise is akin to a not-for-profit firm in terms of its goals and impact and is similar to a for-profit firm in terms of its resource management, operational efficiency, and risk taking.[8] Thus, both non-profit organisations that become entrepreneurial by setting up revenue generating business units to earn income towards supporting their social mission and for-profit ventures that adopt social goals and integrate greater levels of social responsibility into their operations are social enterprises (refer to Figure I.1).

This book presents a collection of case studies that demonstrate the important role played by ten social enterprises in driving inclusive growth in Asia's emerging economies. An adaptation of Kim Alter's hybrid spectrum model helps to highlight and illustrate that the key difference among these social enterprises lies in their primary purpose of existence, and hence they occupy either the left-hand side or the right-hand side on the socio-economic dimension.[9]

Those organisations for which the social mission is the primary purpose, with the commercial operations as the means to achieve sustainability, occupy the left-hand side. Examples of such enterprises are showcased in

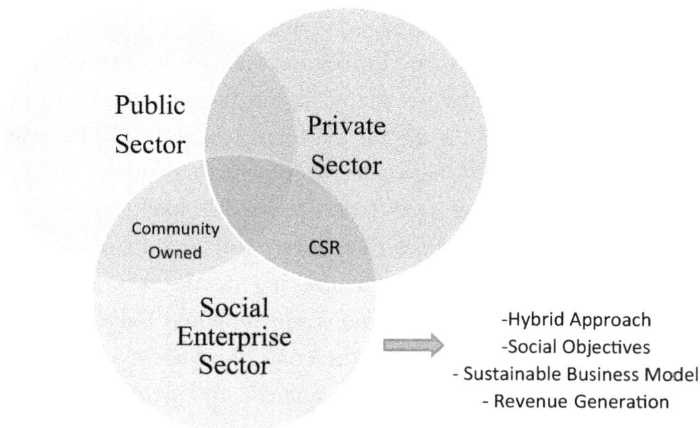

Figure I.1 Social Enterprise Sector

Source: The World Bank, "Emerging Social Enterprise Ecosystems in East and South African Countries" May 2017, https://openknowledge.worldbank.org/bitstream/handle/10986/26672/115052-WP-P152203-PUBLIC-AfricaSEEcosystemMay.pdf?sequence=1.

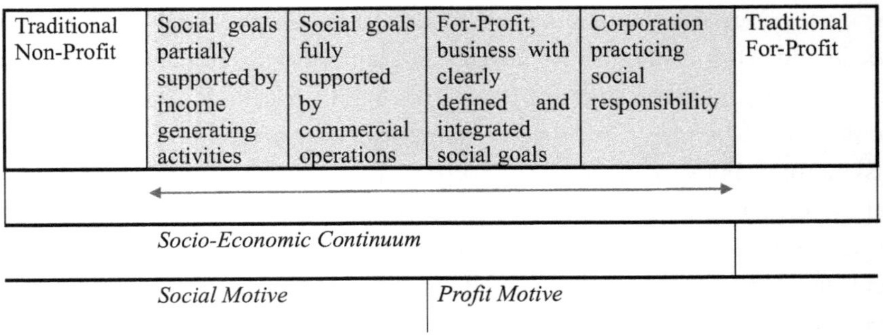

Figure 1.2 Social Enterprise Spectrum
Source: Adapted from Kim Alter, "Social Enterprise Typology", Virtue Ventures, www.4lenses.org/setypology/hybrid-spectrum.

the case studies on ECHOsi, Juntos Global, Yangon Bakehouse, Bettr Barista, and BOP Hub. ECHOsi, a non-profit foundation, works to empower women micro-entrepreneurs in the Philippines, Juntos Global works towards inculcating savings habits among unbanked American residents to develop savings habits, and Yangon Bakehouse provides employability and life skills to the disadvantaged women in Myanmar and supports its social goal by running a commercial restaurant and catering business. Like Yangon Bakehouse, Bettr Barista too provides disadvantaged women and youth in Singapore with barista skills for employability and emotional and physical training for their psychological wellbeing and runs many for-profit businesses to sustain the social endeavour. BOP Hub, a digital platform, connects social enterprises and other stakeholders in the region to promote knowledge sharing and collaboration for serving the BoP population more effectively.

On the other hand, enterprises that pursue social value creation to support their primary purpose of profit making occupy the right-hand side of the dimension. The case studies on iCare Benefits, Fullerton, SureCash, Veriown, and Homage highlight how the creation of social capital and social networks is critical to driving business growth and demand. iCare creates social value for migrant workers in Vietnam by providing them with zero-interest financial services and thus facilitates availability of a productive and loyal workforce for their employers. Fullerton and SureCash are microfinance enterprises catering to the financial needs of the rural poor in Myanmar and Bangladesh, respectively, and in the process benefit from additional revenue and cost savings. Veriown, through its technologically advanced three-in-one solution, provides rural households in India easy access to electricity, the Internet, and financial services at low prices with its flexible usage-based payment model. This has enabled the company to tap into the huge unmet demand of a large consumer segment hitherto inaccessible. Homage, a tech start-up, addresses the healthcare challenge faced by the ageing population in Singapore by connecting the elderly with caregivers for on-demand home care services.

The social enterprises discussed in this book can also be structured along the two key dimensions given by Martin and Osberg (2007)'s framework (as shown in Figure I.3), based on the nature of the social action (direct versus indirect) and the scale of its outcome (local community versus society).

While the authors' model highlights the role of a social enterprise vis-à-vis other social organisations, it can also be used to enumerate the similarities and differences among the social enterprises pursuing individual paths of evolution. Furthermore, the duo point out,

> *It is tempting to think that social entrepreneurs are extraordinary individuals who are capable of connecting all the dots in a flash of insight or a killer strategy, people who were born with the talent for solutions or the perseverance to see them through, but in real life, it is not as straightforward as that. Each story involves a journey, often these begin with the recognition of injustice or suffering.*[10]

Nature of Action		**Outcome**	
		Extant System Maintained and Improved	**New Equilibrium Created and Sustained**
	Direct	*Social service provision*	*Social entrepreneurship*
	Indirect	*None*	*Social activism*

Figure 1.3 Pure Forms of Social Engagement

Source: Roger L. Martin and Sally Osberg, "Social Entrepreneurship: The Case for Definition", Stanford Social Innovation Review, Vol. 5, Issue 2, 2007, pp. 28-39, https://ssir.org/articles/entry/social_entrepreneurship_the_case_for_definition.

Case studies on iCare, Fullerton, Yangon Bakehouse, Bettr Barista, SureCash, and Veriown illustrate how these enterprises cater directly to the needs of their respective local communities. iCare, Fullerton, and SureCash address the financial needs of the population; Veriown provides an alternative source of energy to Indian households, while Yangon Bakehouse and Bettr Barista create employment opportunities for the women in Myanmar and Singapore, respectively.

On the other hand, the case studies on Great Women, Homage, Juntos Global, and BoP Hub present how these organisations indirectly help the poor, unbanked, or elderly through the provision of a messaging platform, client-matching services, or intermediary marketplaces. While Great Women and Homage highlight works of social entrepreneurs within their local communities (the Philippines and Singapore, respectively), the impact of Juntos Global and BoP Hub is more far reaching, as their scope extends to the whole of Southeast Asia.

The essence of each case study is shared in the following brief descriptions, while the conclusion at the end of the book provides an explanation of the social value creation and draws out the lessons that can be learned, and un-learned, from it.

Chapter summaries

Chapter 1

Poverty remains a significant issue in developing countries. In Vietnam, some households cannot afford to buy basic electrical appliances without having to resort to borrowing money at high interest rates. The "iCare Benefits: Assisting Low-Income Retail Consumers in Vietnam" case illustrates how iCare Benefits (iCare), a social enterprise established to help low-income workers, made lending more affordable by providing interest-free instalment plans.

The case demonstrates how social enterprises are different from for-profit organisations and not-for-profit organisations (NPOs). As a purpose- and profit-driven social enterprise, iCare is less reliant on fundraising as compared to NPOs, and its success hinges on whether it achieves its social mission, unlike for-profit organisations whose corporate social responsibility initiatives are largely public relations exercises.

Under iCare's innovative retail model, it secures loans from partner financial institutions at reasonable rates and offers individual interest-free loans to migrant workers in agreement with their employers who adopt the iCare benefits package. Thus, the employees value the employer as a company that helps and supports them. Upon fulfilling the basic physiological needs of the migrant workers, iCare could move on to address their higher-level needs.

Chapter 2

In Myanmar, underprivileged segments of the society are generally unable to access financial services. "Fullerton Myanmar: Delivering Financial Inclusion through Social Impact and Technology" describes how Fullerton Finance (Myanmar) Company Limited ('Fullerton Myanmar'), a microfinance institution, identified the opportunity to educate locals on managing their finances by offering a three-in-one bundled product comprising a loan, a savings account, and a micro-insurance policy.

At Fullerton Myanmar, technology played a key role in bringing significant benefits to the company and its clients. The enterprise benefited from increased revenue, cost savings, fraud reduction, and improved client service, while its clients enjoyed personal cost savings, faster loan disbursement, and lower interest rates. However, there were also hurdles to overcome, such as high costs, lengthy implementation timelines, lack of supporting infrastructure, and customer resistance to new technologies. This case serves as a reminder to microfinance institutions to carefully weigh the costs and benefits of introducing technological innovations to rural communities in developing nations.

Chapter 3

Women play a particularly important role in social entrepreneurship, not only as social entrepreneurs but also in championing women's empowerment in conservative Asian societies. In the case of "Yangon Bakehouse: A Social Enterprise in Myanmar," the enterprise strives to lend a hand to the destitute and the underprivileged by taking on unskilled and uneducated women as culinary apprentices who would typically work for its restaurant and catering business upon completing their apprenticeship. As a commercial revenue-generating business, Yangon Bakehouse was able to break free from the restrictions imposed by donors on non-government organisations and did not have to depend on the generosity of donors.

This case exemplifies how a social enterprise might descend into a financial crisis while trying to fulfil its mission of pursuing social inclusion of poor women. Sustaining growth after experiencing initial success was challenging, given the absence of experienced management, the lack of legal recognition for social enterprises, and the low level of government support for small-scale entrepreneurs. To close the financial–social return gap, Yangon Bakehouse would need to make use of available financing options, such as quasi-equity debt and direct-public offering. Besides financial capital, the building of social capital was equally important. To this end, the measures undertaken by Yangon Bakehouse included delivering training programmes with a dual focus on both technical and soft skills, as well as monthly remuneration, counselling support, and job placements for the apprentices, usually within Yangon.

Chapter 4

Continuing with the theme of women's empowerment, the case of "SureCash: Promoting Financial Inclusion in Bangladesh" relates the opening of mobile bank accounts for the mothers of 13 million poor Bangladeshi students so that education stipends for their children could be credited directly into their accounts instead of letting them hold onto cash. By taking part in the government-led Primary Education Stipend Program, SureCash has taken a significant step towards enabling unbanked women in rural Bangladesh to become financially included. Financial inclusion, as demonstrated through the SureCash case, benefits individuals and families, as they gain access to financial services, but it also empowers entire communities to drive economic growth collectively.

However, as a mobile financial service provider in a developing economy, SureCash has to manage the key elements within the end-user, institutional, and market environments. Moreover, SureCash operates in an oligopolistic market (dominated by a few large firms), and in such circumstances, it is perhaps best to adopt a niche market competitive strategy. To be successful in a niche market, SureCash will need to ensure it meets the following criteria: high market demand, low degree of competition, and high income potential.

Chapter 5

Despite facing a multitude of difficulties under less-than-ideal conditions, social enterprises have demonstrated their ability to think out of the box. In the case study of "Veriown: Connecting the Invisible Woman in India," the founder was deeply moved by a video of a young woman working under poor lighting conditions at night. This drove him to set up Veriown, a solar service provider, with the primary objective to provide solar energy as a cleaner and safer alternate source of electricity, in place of kerosene, a polluter and far-inferior fuel commonly used in India. On top of offering an environmentally friendly power source, he observed that poverty-stricken rural Indians lacked access to connectivity and finance, thus prompting him to partner with telecom provider Vodafone and non-banking financial company DMI to package telecom and micro-loan services with Veriown's core offering of supplying electricity.

In discussing the business model of a social enterprise that targets rural or poor communities, the Veriown case introduces the concepts of value creation and value delivery. It offers a unique business model that innovatively bundles three services into one offering, along with a 'pay-as-you-consume' service. In order to bring about value creation, Veriown developed an efficient and cost-effective value chain by leveraging existing infrastructure, collaborating with the local community, and adopting a do-it-yourself model where customers could implement the solution themselves. In addition, Veriown was able to maximise value delivery through an efficient last-mile distribution network through its partnership with Vodafone and DMI.

Chapter 6

The case on "Great Women: Integrating Micro-Entrepreneurs into the Regional Value Chain" highlights ECHOsi, a non-profit foundation set up by three women with the aim to empower female micro-entrepreneurs in the Philippines. ECHOsi offered services to link up female micro-producers to their market and supported them in refining their product offerings and expanding their client base. It was of immense assistance to these women micro-entrepreneurs, many of whom were small-scale producers unaware of market expectations and would have faced much difficulty if left unassisted.

The co-founders believed that when women were economically empowered, most of their earnings were reinvested in the business or spent on nutrition, education, and health of the family. Hence, they decided to focus on women micro-entrepreneurs to create the desired social impact. The Great Women case highlights the importance of women micro-entrepreneurs' contribution to sustainable economic development, especially in Southeast Asia, where working women are more likely to be self employed than working men. Despite multiple challenges, the co-founders eventually overcame the issue of gender constraints that hindered Filipino women's access to business networks.

Chapter 7

In the case on "Homage: Harnessing Technology to Tackle Singapore's Ageing Challenges," the founders of the tech start-up Homage observed a gap between the high demand and low supply in Singapore's elder home care services market. To meet the ageing population's healthcare needs, Homage provided on-demand home care services ranging from nursing care and assisted daily living to therapy. Its mobile app platform connects non-practising healthcare professionals and allied caregivers to the elderly in need of professional caregiving and their families.

As co-founder Tee explained,

> *There was this vast untapped workforce that valued flexibility, and there were these households with elders that needed caregivers on demand, just like software-as-a-service (SaaS). We wanted to empower the untapped manpower to become micro-entrepreneurs to trade their time, expertise and service on-demand, on their terms, and build a meaningful career for themselves while the seniors and their families had reliable access to efficient and trained caregivers at an affordable price. Technology would help us overcome the inefficiencies found in conventional services.*

Homage's innovation addresses the increasing homecare needs of the elderly using technology as an enabler of social innovation.

In order for innovation to transform society, systemic change is necessary. The case explores three key drivers, innovation environment, innovation process, and innovation adoption, which affect Homage's potential to effect systemic change. In addition, the case illustrates the critical role that grants and private capital play at various stages of the innovation lifecycle and the strategies that Homage can adopt for scaling social innovations.

Chapter 8

Despite the prevalence of freeware messaging apps such as WhatsApp and WeChat, the case on "Juntos Global: Deploying Human-Centred Design to Motivate the Newly Banked" explains that short message service (SMS) could also be a useful mobile communication tool to cultivate good savings habits among newly banked individuals in Southeast Asia, for whom banking and saving are still novelties. Using behavioural science strategies based on human-centred design (HCD) principles, Juntos facilitated the building of trusting relationships between financial service providers and the users of its platform. Co-founder Ben Knelman explained, "It's simple to teach users through SMS how to check their bank balance from their phone. . . . Users may feel encouraged by the amount they see on that little, black screen, knowing they are slowly and steadily approaching their goal."

The Juntos Global case introduces behavioural economics theories such as the EAST (easy, attractive, social and timely) model utilised by the social enterprise in its attempt to influence customer adoption. In addition, the crafting of Juntos' messaging is based on HCD principles that were intended to help NPOs design products and services with the end user in mind. The case also reminds readers that social inclusion and financial inclusion are inextricably linked; therefore, social entrepreneurs should pay attention to the information and communicative dimensions of social inclusion when promoting financial inclusion for low-income communities.

Chapter 9

In the case study "Bettr Barista: A Shot at Better Lives," Pamela Chng, the founder of Singapore-based Bettr Barista, believes that a workplace cannot exist aloof from society's challenges and that companies need to be accountable for their contributions to society. Bettr Barista is her attempt to go beyond the pure profit motive and improve the lives of marginalised women and youth in the city-state. The enterprise offers a four-month-long holistic programme, equipping them with job skills as a barista. Bettr Barista's large menu of for-profit businesses, including internationally certified speciality coffee education and training workshops, coffee roastery, retail coffee outlets and mobile brew bars, supports and sustains its social mission.

The case highlights the challenge in maintaining the balance between financial and social goals, as this drives most of the decisions taken by the company, be its value chain or the key stakeholders. The social role, on the one hand, may accord the company a differentiated position in a fragmented and congested industry; on the other hand, it adversely affects the company's productivity and resource utilisation and hence its ability to grow.

Chapter 10

In the final case, "Base of Pyramid Hub: Connecting Solutions," Jack Sim, the founder of Base of Pyramid (BoP) Hub, explains how he intends to cater to the sizeable portion of the global population that is still stuck in poverty and pays a 'poverty penalty' to access everyday use utilities, products, and services. The primary objective of the BoP Hub was to provide professional services to social entrepreneurs catering to the BoP market and help them develop and scale their businesses. However, in addition to the social objectives, the BoP Hub also has economic incentives, as the potential volume in this segment is huge, and it aspires to move into the middle class. As Sim notes,

> *The poor need all kinds of things—like clothing, food, water filters, cooking stoves, vehicles, entertainment products, solar lamps, low cost housing, sanitation, education, healthcare, pharmaceutical products—the list is long. It is for all these needs that social enterprises can come together to provide cost effective solutions that target this strata of buyers.*

The case elaborates on one of the key challenges faced by social entrepreneurs who are designing offerings for the BoP, which is the issue of 'financial sustainability.' Specific to these entrepreneurs who design offerings for very low-income urban neighbourhoods, they face constant funding uncertainty due to short programme timelines, very stringent accountability requirements by their sources of funding, and high expectations of showing results. This case also highlights the larger challenges faced by social enterprises in terms of socio-cultural issues and business scaling and discusses the strategies to address them. It highlights the 'beanstalk' strategy and explains how this is appropriate as a key driver for growth for initiatives like BoP Hub.

The journey continues

With every passing day, we take comfort that social entrepreneurs are working towards the good of others in one way or another. Yet social enterprises continue to grapple with the two seemingly contradictory objectives of serving the social needs of the community while having to achieve financial sustainability. This book intends to shed some light on what makes these enterprises tick.

As the protagonists in the cases continue their social entrepreneurship journeys, may they be inspired by the words of Simon Sinek, a motivational speaker and author of the book *Start with Why: How Great Leaders Inspire Everyone to Take Action*: "Don't quit. Never give up trying to build the world you can see, even if others can't see it. Listen to your drum and your drum only. It's the one that makes the sweetest sound."[11]

Notes

1 Weiyan Zhou, Xiaobin Zhu, Tianxue Qiu, Ruijun Yuan, Jingya Chen, and Tongkui Chen, "China Social Enterprise and Impact Investment Report", March 2013, http://serc-china.org/attachments/article/542/China percent20Social percent20Enterprise percent20and percent20Impact percent20Investment percent20Report.pdf.

2 Daryl Poon, "The Emergence and Development of Social Enterprise Sectors", *Social Impact Research Experience (SIRE)*, 8 (2011), http://repository.upenn.edu/sire/8, accessed September 2017.

3 Tomomi Kikuchi, "Social Enterprises' Rise in Asia Amid Scepticism", *Nikkei Asian Review*, 27 December 2017, https://asia.nikkei.com/Spotlight/The-Big-Story/Social-enterprises-rise-in-Asia-amid-skepticism2.

4 Lily Odarno, *1.2 Billion People Lack Electricity. Increasing Supply Alone Won't Fix the Problem*, World Resources Institute, March 2017, www.wri.org/blog/2017/03/12-billion-people-lack-electricity-increasing-supply-alone-wont-fix-problem.

5 The World Bank, "Social Inclusion", www.worldbank.org/en/topic/social-inclusion.

6 Muhammad Yunus, *Building Social Business: The New Kind of Capitalism That Serves Humanity's Most Pressing Needs*, Public Affairs, 2010, https://sun-connect-news.org/fileadmin/DATEIEN/Dateien/New/BUILDING-SOCIAL-BUSINESS-MUHAMMAD-YUNUS.pdf.

7 Howard Thomas and Yuwa Hedrick-Wong, *Inclusive Growth: The Global Challenges of Social Inequality and Financial Inclusion*, Bingley, UK: Emerald Group Publishing, 2019; Roger L. Martin and Sally Osberg, *Social Entrepreneurship: The Case for Definition*, Stanford Social Innovation Review, 2007, https://ssir.org/articles/entry/social_entrepreneurship_the_case_for_definition.

8 Christian Seelos and Johanna Mair, "Social Entrepreneurship: Creating New Business Models to Serve the Poor", *Business Horizons*, 48(3) (2005): 241–246.

9 Kim Alter, *Social Enterprise Typology*, Virtue Ventures, www.4lenses.org/setypology/hybrid-spectrum.

10 Roger L. Martin and Sally Osberg, *Getting Beyond Better: How Social Entrepreneurship Works*, Boston, Massachusetts, U.S.: Harvard Business Review Press, 2015.

11 Simon Sinek, "The Left-Siders", https://simonsinek.com/discover/the-left-siders.

1

ICARE BENEFITS: ASSISTING LOW-INCOME RETAIL CONSUMERS IN VIETNAM

Howard Thomas, Aurobindo Ghosh, and CW Chan

Poverty remains a significant issue in developing countries. In Vietnam, some households cannot afford to buy basic electrical appliances without having to resort to borrowing money at high interest rates. The iCare Benefits: Assisting Low Income Retail Consumers in Vietnam case illustrates how iCare Benefits (iCare), a social enterprise established to help low-income workers, made finance more inclusive by providing interest-free instalment plans.

The case demonstrates how social enterprises are different from for-profit organisations and not-for-profit organisations (NPOs). As a purpose- and profit-driven social enterprise, iCare is less reliant on fundraising as compared to NPOs, and its success hinges on whether it achieves its social mission, unlike for-profit organisations whose corporate social responsibility initiatives are largely public relations exercises. Under iCare's innovative retail model, it secures loans from partner financial institutions at reasonable rates and offers individual interest-free loans to migrant workers in agreement with their employers who adopt the iCare benefits package. Thus, the employees value the employer as a company that helps and supports them. Upon fulfilling the basic physiological needs of migrant workers, iCare can move on to address their higher-level needs.

Trung Dung, the founder of iCare Benefits, a social enterprise established to aid low-income workers, was born in the south of Vietnam, a seafaring nation located in South East Asia. From a young

DOI: 10.4324/9781003203582-2

age, Trung experienced poverty, as his father was interned as a political prisoner in the aftermath of the Vietnam War. He made ends meet through fishing and peddling fruits. In search of a better life, he tried to escape to the United States on a fishing boat but was caught and diverted to an Indonesian refugee camp. He spent a year in camp before receiving authorisation to go to the United States. Despite having no money and speaking little English, he hoped life there would be preferable to the one he had left.

In the United States, Trung took on double the usual university courseload while working odd jobs to send money home. Despite having to brush up on his English, he decided to study mathematics and computer science at the University of Massachusetts in Boston. "Back in Vietnam, there was no future," said Trung, "The only way to move up is to get an education. Here, the whole world opened up to me." He got a job at Open Market, an e-commerce software company, before he started his own businesses. His most successful project was OnDisplay Corporation, a software development company that powered e-commerce platforms. It was eventually acquired by Vignette, a content management company, for US$1.7 billion. After experiencing financial success, Trung wanted to give back to the community that had been a big influence during his formative years.

Vietnam economic environment

Vietnam had been a French colony until the independence movement ended in victory at Dien Bien Phu in 1954. However, the ceasefire negotiated at the Geneva Accords resulted in a temporary partition of Vietnam. Civil war between the communist North and the anti-communist South was almost inevitable. When hostilities resumed later that year, the United States backed the South to prevent Vietnam's neighbours from falling under communist influence. Support from ordinary Americans ebbed as the protracted war inflicted many casualties. After widespread protests, the US government eventually ended American involvement in the war in 1973. Vietnam's infrastructure and economy had been decimated by war. Critical infrastructure had been destroyed by heavy bombings, and South Vietnam could no longer count on US aid. The government made an economic plan based on the communist principles of collectivisation, the pooling of resources under state control, and land reform.

The Vietnam economy had been heavily dependent on agriculture and exported commodities, such as coffee, pepper, and rubber. During the decade following the war, the Vietnamese government's failure to meet modest food production goals led to a shift in economic policy. Following the failure of collectivisation, the government instituted a policy in the mid-1980s of 'doi moi,' or 'economic renovation,' whereby the country discarded central planning to embrace free-market principles. While the state retained substantial influence on the economy, from 1990, Vietnam experienced one of the fastest global GDP per capita growth rates due to an expanding manufacturing sector.[1]

Global manufacturers took advantage of an abundance of cheap labour in Vietnam to move out of an increasingly expensive China. While the growing economy lifted many Vietnamese out of abject poverty, the growth of manufacturing also triggered rural migration to urban areas. Trung spoke about the search for a better standard of living,

> *A worker can typically make US$1 a day as a farmer but that income is not regular. As a factory worker, his or her income improves to US$5 to US$10 a day. That is a significant improvement over what they could earn in the rural area.*

However, urban living was also more expensive. The many migrant workers who resided at the bottom of the pyramid had barely any savings. An estimated 39 million out of 90 million Vietnamese earned US$5 or less a day.[2]

With limited purchasing power, the retail environment was daunting for such migrant workers. Typically, wholesalers would facilitate market activity by purchasing goods from manufacturers and reselling them to retailers. Wholesalers would buy goods in bulk and arrange the transportation of the goods to and from their warehouses before distributing it at a mark-up to retailers. Retailers would attract end consumers by renting brick-and-mortar stores in locations with high traffic or spending on advertising. The manufacturing boom resulted in the clustering of migrant workers in factories located on the outskirts of major cities, far from any stores.

Furthermore, low-income workers could not obtain loans from financial institutions for big-ticket items. Banks felt that the administrative costs of due diligence required to make small loans was prohibitive. A common alternative was to use informal savings groups known as *hui*. Pawel Gorski, deputy head, Strategic Marketing Department of iCare, explained how the system worked,

> *Traditionally, people who know each other, relatives, neighbours or friends, form groups and everybody contributes some amount to the common fund. Then there is a bidding, where the person who bid the highest interest rate will be able to cash out as a loan and then pay interest to the rest of the group. Of course, there is a risk of actually losing the money if one of the members of the group suddenly disappears or is not able to pay. Therefore, they form groups with people they trust and keep each other accountable.*

If the group lacked sufficient savings, the workers had to borrow money from the black market at exorbitant interest rates to meet expenses for basic goods.

Enabling change

Trung was aware of the difficulties the marginalised population faced in managing their meagre savings and wanted to introduce modern financial technology (FinTech) to the region. In 2007, he returned to Vietnam to start Mobivi, an electronic payment service, to provide financial solutions to consumers in Vietnam. The service was meant to reduce transaction costs and increase convenience for users. After speaking to merchants and labour unions, Trung realised that the demand for such a service was low, as it was difficult to convince people to switch from using cash to an e-payment service.

Conversations with employers, global manufacturers and financial institutions led Trung to discover that the lack of access to consumer financing made it difficult for factory workers to participate in the traditional retail sector. Gorski explained,

> *The workers were able to express what they needed. If we could provide access to a fridge, a TV, a smartphone, a fan or a bed mattress, that would be something really useful. So the founders realised by chance, from talking and discussing with workers, trade unions, and global brands representatives, that, beginning with the factories, millions of migrant workers had a huge unmet need.*

Additionally, migrant workers were burdened by rental commitments and had little left over for essential products. They also needed to travel an average of 45 minutes to find a market or retail store. The lack of a fridge required frequent trips to the market to buy food. The cooking process also had to be precise to prevent wastage. The absence of a mattress could cause physical pain and disrupted sleep that would affect a person's work.

Trung wanted to provide an innovative retail service to redress the situation. Eventually, he made a breakthrough. He decided to relaunch the business as a for-profit social enterprise that handled employee benefits and developed a third-party employee benefits programme that would help low-income migrant workers afford basic goods. iCare would work with partner organisations to aid low-income workers at the bottom of the pyramid. It would undertake retail functions to enable migrant workers to access essential life-changing products and services. While Trung's aim was not to maximise profits, he endeavoured to operate without any handouts, as he believed that it was harder to plan in a company that was dependent on varying amounts of donations annually. Furthermore, fundraising efforts required time and energy that could be put towards other issues.

Building a community

Using an innovative retail model, iCare provided workers with zero-interest instalment payment options for up to six months. Trung forged a collaborative ecosystem with his partners that permitted the social enterprise to operate without donations. Instead of renting a physical storefront in a high-traffic area, he decided to approach large factories, and a partnership development team was set up to persuade them to sign onto the iCare platform. These factories housed large clusters of migrant workers, who were iCare's target segment. Employers were largely supportive of the initiative, as a successful benefits programme would help with employee retention; only workers with tenure of at least a year would be allowed to register for the programme. Creating a more comfortable home environment would also result in greater productivity at work. These incentives were expected to increase worker engagement and reduce turnover costs for the factories. Gorski explained the process,

The first step is to enter into a partnership agreement with the factory where the workers are employed. The team will have to collaborate with the factory management and the labour union before we are able to serve the workers. Subsequently, registration for workers in the programme is voluntary, and if they choose to participate, they will require approval from their supervisor.

Collaborating with factories provided iCare with a captive market and allowed it to take advantage of economies of scale. The iCare retail process enabled workers to order from an e-commerce app, telesales staff, or directly from the sales team when they visited. Consumers could place their orders through an online platform and payment could be deducted from payroll.

Manufacturers

The next step was to work with companies that manufactured basic consumer durable goods and see how they could help migrant workers get access to their products. Many workers left their hometowns without many belongings, and household necessities could cost more than a month's salary. Gorski discussed the low-income market,

Items like refrigerators, washing machines, smartphones, are things that we take for granted in our lives. However, when workers move to industrial zones, they don't have any of these and it's difficult for them to afford or even get access to these goods.

The iCare team negotiated with manufacturers for distribution contracts. These manufacturers could reach an untapped market by coordinating with iCare and increase their sales and brand awareness. The manufacturing companies would bring sample products to factories or allow workers to browse catalogues to place their orders and make deliveries to their homes. Gorski explained how iCare managed to collaborate with some of the biggest consumer brands,

We managed to link up with some of the biggest consumer brands, including Samsung and Panasonic. Our value proposition is to help them expand their reach, and to increase their sales. Currently, Samsung products are nearly 50 percent of all the sales on the iCare Benefits platform. That is an opportunity for Samsung to sell to a segment that previously was unable to afford their products.

Additionally, the partnership with manufacturers allowed iCare to save on inventory costs, as goods were delivered on demand.

Financial institutions

The biggest issue for workers was the lack of access to financing. These workers were neglected by banks due to their lack of collateral and the high risk of default on loans. Gorski spoke about the market segment,

> *We target workers who are making between US$150–400 a month. These workers usually end up taking black market loans for consumer products that cost more than US$150. Incidentally, more than 80 percent of the people we serve are female factory workers.*

iCare decided to work with financial institutions to absorb the interest fees and offer consumers interest-free six-month instalment plans for their purchases. The interest-free loans offered to iCare members were not without risks to the social enterprise. iCare was vulnerable to both micro and macro risks by undertaking the role of a financial service provider. Nevertheless, iCare could negotiate lower interest rates with the banks compared to an individual migrant worker.

Since 2014, iCare has successfully helped low-income migrant workers afford basic consumer durable goods in a safe and risk-free manner. Earlier, borrowers had to risk damaging their creditworthiness and relationships if they could not repay loans. The black market was even more unforgiving. Loan sharks would sometimes take items such as motorcycles as collateral for loans given at extortionate interest rates and make physical threats or even resort to violence to ensure repayment. After the iCare programme began, the practice of borrowing from other sources dropped dramatically. Gorski was proud that iCare had undeniably changed the borrowing habits of members (refer to Table 1.1),

> *Previously, we found out workers would usually borrow from family and friends, the black market, and pawn shops at high interest rates. After one year of running the iCare programme in the factories, we conducted the survey with the same question 'how do you get cash for essential products and services?' and we saw that there had been a huge drop in the level of informal lending. So, it eradicated the need to reach out to informal lending because there was another option that was safer and less costly.*

Table 1.1 Survey on Migrant Workers' Financing Sources

Year	iCare Benefits	Friends & Family	Black Market	Pawn Assets
2014	0.2	64.2%	18.3%	14.1%
2015	64.1%	14.7%	2.5%	1.9%

Trung received positive feedback from many stakeholders. iCare members could purchase essential goods without travelling long distances and thus spend more time with their families. In a survey taken by the factories, many workers in the programme felt more productive at work—92 percent felt their quality of life had improved, 81 percent were more satisfied at work and 68 percent said they could buy things that were previously unaffordable. It was estimated that they saved an average of US$226 in costs and 12 working days in time annually. This was the time they would have otherwise needed to take off from work. Employers were able to increase their employee retention rate, and manufacturers that had no prior access to this market were able to increase their sales.

Expanding the programme

Trung was buoyed by the initial success and felt he could provide a broader suite of offerings to suit the shifting needs of workers. As living standards improved, Vietnamese consumers started to pay more attention to healthcare and education. Local society held academic credentials in high esteem, and parents considered educating their children investments for the future. Most workers were interested in options that would help them save on school supplies for their children. Additionally, more than two thirds of workers did not have any money saved for emergencies, and around half were interested in more comprehensive health check-ups for their families. The healthcare system administered by the government had been widely criticised as inefficient and underfunded, leading consumers to seek treatment overseas.

By developing partnerships with more manufacturers, service providers, and development organisations, iCare aimed to address the household needs of factory workers more comprehensively. The provision of access to essential goods was the first of four pillars termed 'comfort living.' In 2016, iCare

Table 1.2 The Pillars of iCare Benefits

Pillars	*Description*
Comfort Living	iCare Benefits members can instantly afford essential products with a no-interest payment plan.
Healthy Living	Employees can gain access to essential health services and medicine to enhance their wellbeing.
Smart Living	iCare Benefits provides access to essential knowledge, education, and virtual training for members and families.
Prosperous Living	Discover new opportunities to access personal finance tools, loans, and saving plans.

added three more pillars to their benefits programme: healthy living, smart living, and prosperous living (refer to Table 1.2).

Trung spoke about the enhanced programme offering,

> *iCare Benefits as an employee benefits programme is designed to improve the standard of living of factory workers. It enables workers and their families to get access to many essential products and services in four areas: household goods, healthcare services, educational training and basic financial services. A factory worker may find it difficult to afford these necessities because they might cost more than a month's salary. The biggest difference is iCare Benefits allows a worker to buy what they need and pay in up to six equal monthly instalments with zero interest.*

Healthy living

Medical emergencies represented the biggest issue, given the lack of savings. A sudden onset of illnesses could affect the ability of workers to do their jobs and require them to take distress loans at usurious rates. Instead of providing healthcare when workers got sick, iCare's programme focused on prevention. The 'healthy living' scheme helped to ensure good health and promote wellbeing for all ages. Many workers lacked access to information about infectious diseases. For example, the human papillomavirus (HPV) was a common disease in Vietnam, but most workers were unaware of the virus and its associated health risks. Workers usually had to resort to borrowing large amounts of money to pay for medical bills if they contracted it. Trung spoke about the pilot project to help workers take preventative healthcare measures,

> *An example of the healthcare services provided is the HPV vaccine to prevent cervical cancer in young women. A single one-time payment for the vaccine is extremely hard for them. We work with a partner to make the cost less prohibitive by permitting a nine-month instalment plan. Suddenly we see a significant number of them lining up to get inoculated.*

The pilot run involved five factories, with 660 workers attending workshops conducted by iCare. Eventually 381 workers and their family members were inoculated against the disease. In addition, iCare members saved US$58 and 13 hours of wait time each by participating in iCare's vaccination programme rather than going to a clinic. Due to the positive response from workers, iCare gradually introduced health check-ups, female reproductive health services, and access to contraceptives.

Smart living

The 'smart living' scheme sought to promote lifelong learning opportunities for workers and ensure quality education for their children. The first educational project for workers was around safety. A trial run introduced two workplace safety videos to 249 workers. The format of short and visually attractive videos was well received by the workers and helped them retain the information shown in the videos. Subsequently, the workers scored 94 percent in the fire safety test and 81 percent in the chemical safety test. Through their partnership with UNICEF, iCare also disseminated information on basic sanitation and breastfeeding directly to the workers for free.

Even more important was the cost of education for the workers' children. Trung discussed how the cost of education was a problem,

> *We want to help workers and their families get access to education and vocational training. I have learned that when school starts in September, many parents get into debt because they borrow to purchase school supplies, books, PCs and tuition fees. Computer lessons for children may cost US$20 and parents are more willing to spend if offered a six-month instalment plan.*

To help parents save time and money, iCare prepared school packages with notebooks, pens, and other tools for parents to buy.

Prosperous living

The last pillar, 'Prosperous Living,' was started in anticipation of workers achieving higher living standards and working towards promotions in their professions. Through this scheme, workers would have access to basic financial services such as savings, insurance, and cash loans. For workers with brighter prospects, iCare worked with a partner bank to offer a simple cash advance, with the loan to be repaid on the day when the next salary was credited. With proper planning, workers would have the financial freedom to spend not out of necessity but out of choice.

Looking ahead

With the support of the community, iCare was able to provide consumer goods to low-income workers. Without donations, iCare relied on profits to sustain its social mission. Gorski elaborated on the retail business model, "iCare earns profits on the margin between selling at the retail price and buying at the wholesale price." Compared to traditional retailers, iCare saved over 5 percent on various costs. It saved on advertising costs by collaborating with factories on their employee benefits programmes, on inventory costs as products were directly available through manufacturers, and on rental for offices and storefronts as sales offices were mostly located on company premises.

However, iCare also needed a robust risk management system to mitigate the additional default risks. On a macro level, it had insurance that would cover some of the potential loan defaults. The micro-loans extended by iCare were for shorter durations than the large amounts of money borrowed from financial institutions. It also monitored the industry for mass upheavals, which could lead to job losses and defaults. Since this systematic risk would unfold over a long period of time, iCare would slow its frequency of lending should any warning signs appear. On a micro level, iCare collaborated with factory managers to analyse the enterprise-level database of employers to evaluate the likelihood of termination of individual employees. This pre-selection process would preclude high-risk employees from gaining membership to the programme.

The use of data analytics and strong loan management practices helped sustain iCare's business model, but Trung needed community support for access to continuous sources of credit and consumer products. Thus far, iCare had managed to operate sustainably while creating a win-win situation for everyone in the community. Employers improved their employee retention, product partners increased sales, and financial partners disbursed more loans. Most importantly, low-income workers could improve their standard of living. To continue making a positive social impact, Trung knew that he had to work hard to maintain and expand the community.

Notes

1 Passport, Vietnam: Country Profile, 30 March 2018.

2 Viet Nam News, "Companies Told to Target BoP Market", 6 March 2018, http://vietnamnews.vn/economy/267152/companies-told-to-target-bop-market.html.

2

FULLERTON MYANMAR: DELIVERING FINANCIAL INCLUSION THROUGH SOCIAL IMPACT AND TECHNOLOGY

Howard Thomas and Miguel Angel Soriano

This case is set in 2017, three years after Fullerton Myanmar (FFMCL), a microfinance institution (MFI) in Myanmar, was founded by Fullerton Financial Holdings, a Singapore-based firm that invests and operates financial institutions in Asian emerging markets. Since its inception, FFMCL has established itself as one of the top five MFIs in Myanmar. To achieve its mission of "Enabling Success, Enriching Lives," FFMCL demonstrated tremendous success in providing loans to microenterprises in Myanmar using technology. The company has established an ambitious growth plan of expanding coverage fivefold in the next five years. Given the technological advances related to mobile financial services and big data analytics, what role does technology play in FFCML's plan, and what strategy should the company follow to achieve its plan?

This case offers the readers the chance to explore the underlying dynamics of the microfinance sector in Myanmar and understand the process of planning and setting up a new microfinance business in the country. In addition, they can study the strategy that MFIs could follow in order to scale their operations in a competitive market while helping the poor. Finally, it also provides an opportunity to explore the role of technology in the microfinance sector.

Anindo Mukherjee, head of Integrated Risk Management, and his team at Fullerton Financial Holdings (FFH) reflected on the three-year anniversary

DOI: 10.4324/9781003203582-3

of Fullerton Finance (Myanmar) Company Limited ('Fullerton Myanmar' or FFMCL), founded in 2014. "How quickly time flies," Mukherjee commented. "It feels like it was just yesterday when FFH's leadership made the decision to build a greenfield microfinance institution (MFI) in one of the fastest growing frontier economies in Southeast Asia–Myanmar."

FFMCL was among the top five MFIs in Myanmar in terms of loans outstanding. By the end of 2016, it served 64,000 customers in 18 townships through 14 branches with a total loan portfolio of approximately US$12.8 million.[1] Much of this success was attributed to its raison d'être and ability to leverage the knowledge gained from its strategic investments in India and other parts of Asia, which embodied FFH's mission statement of "Enabling success, enriching lives."

By late 2017, the management team at FFH was looking forward to setting the stage for the next chapter in the FFMCL story. They needed to balance the ambitious goal of expanding coverage fivefold over the next five years with that of staying true to their principles of positive social impact and delivering inclusive financial products and services to the poor and underserved masses. FFH's management team needed to construct a winning strategy to scale up operations, with technology continuing to play an important role in the plan.

Fullerton Financial Holdings

FFH invests in and operates financial institutions in Asian emerging markets, including China, Cambodia, India, Malaysia, and Myanmar. It has also held investments in Indonesia and Vietnam previously. Founded in 2003, it is a wholly owned subsidiary of Temasek, one of the largest investment companies based in Singapore. FFH focuses on offering holistic services to four types of customers: small and medium enterprises (SMEs), self-employed mass market, mass affluent, and mass salaried.

Financial inclusion is at the heart of what FFH does. The company creates innovative, cost-effective methods to service the smallest customer, helping them to achieve their dreams for a better future. FFH provides affordable loans that are accessible to micro, small, and medium entrepreneurs to help them with their businesses. In most cases, these individuals have had no access to a formal bank loan, or if they did, it was too costly or difficult to obtain.

Fullerton Myanmar's mission

FFMCL provides affordable financing, primarily to micro-enterprises in Myanmar. The company's mission of "Enabling Success, Enriching Lives" encapsulated its desired role in the lives of its target customers—women's livelihood groups, small business owners, and the salaried mass market, all of whom are underserved due to the limited reach of banks, as well as the customers' inability to provide collateral for secured loans.

As of the end of 2017, FFMCL was 70 percent owned by FFH, while Capital Diamond Star Group (CDSG), one of the leading conglomerates in Myanmar, and the International Finance Corporation (IFC), the private arm of the World Bank, owned 15 percent each of the shares of the company.

FFMCL employed a two-pronged business model consisting of group loans mainly to women with social guarantees and individual loans to small business owners in both urban and rural locations. Within these two categories, there were multiple sub-products, and the company strived to introduce new products suitable for its customers.

In 2013, Myanmar was not yet open to foreign investors, but it was evident that the country offered significant growth potential and opportunities, as there was a large unmet need for access to financial services and financial products to its population. Specifically, there were 30 million adults in Myanmar, or approximately 77 percent of the population, who were unserved by formal lending institutions and were potential customers of MFIs.

The business model

FFH considered various modes of entry into the Myanmar market and finally decided to start its own operations from scratch. There were a few reasons for selecting this alternative. The Myanmar government did not allow foreign entities to invest in local financial institutions at that time. Second, the acquisition of an existing financial institution in Myanmar posed significant risks, mainly related to limited knowledge of loan portfolios of these institutions and unknown management teams. FFH believed that entering into a greenfield MFI would give it full control over its operations. Moreover, the company had extensive prior experience in setting up new operations in emerging markets and had developed a standardised approach and set of procedures in setting up new financial institutions. All this could be usefully applied in their entry into Myanmar.

In May 2014, FFMCL was awarded a one-year licence by the government to operate in 12 townships in Myanmar. The company performed a detailed survey of the different locations, meeting and interviewing village leaders, and assessing the credit history and needs of the population within a 5–10-kilometre radius, as well as the market potential. This survey was part of FFH's standardised process of setting up new businesses, known as the Branch/Catchment Evaluation Report.

During the start-up phase, FFH seconded its domain experts to Myanmar. This included some staff from Fullerton India, who had helped to establish the lending policies and operational processes of Fullerton Myanmar. In the first two years of operations, the FFH team conducted regular reviews to ensure that the practices were well understood and executed. The knowledge transfer from the Fullerton managers, as well as using a standardised process to set up the MFI, were key to allowing Fullerton Myanmar to start issuing loans quickly, within five months of obtaining its microfinance licence. This was done in record time relative to other operations that FFH had set up. For instance, it took them more than a year and a half to set up operations in India and about nine months to set up operations in Cambodia.

By August 2015, FFMCL had acquired over 26,000 new customers and opened 12 branches in three provinces, creating 275 new jobs and disbursing US$3.6 million in loans. By October 2018, after four years of operations, the company had demonstrated significant growth, serving 130,000 active borrowers in Myanmar, and had disbursed more than US$110 million in loans.

Myanmar: the 'New Frontier'

Myanmar, the second largest country in Southeast Asia in terms of land mass, is a densely forested, largely rural country located between India and Thailand. Following its independence from the British in 1948, the country experienced prolonged fragility from 1962 to 2011. During this time, an oppressive military junta wielded absolute power in the face of international censure and sanctions—resulting in decades of stagnation, mismanagement, and isolation.[2]

It was only in 2011 when political reforms started to come into effect that measures were adopted to overhaul the economy and reintegrate Myanmar with the rest of the world. However, serious economic challenges remained in dealing with issues such as inadequate infrastructure, underdeveloped human resources, and inadequate access to capital.

The banking and microfinance sectors in Myanmar

In 2015, the financial sector in Myanmar was still small and undeveloped. Compared to other Association of Southeast Asian Nations (ASEAN) countries, the contribution of Myanmar's banking sector to the economy was limited. For instance, Myanmar's banking assets-to-GDP ratio of 49 percent was the lowest among its ASEAN peers.[3] Nevertheless, the banking sector was one of the fastest growing in the region, with an asset base growth rate of 18 percent over the previous three years.[4] Access to financial services was severely limited, as reflected by the low outstanding loans-to-GDP ratio of 4.7 percent and deposits-to-GDP ratio of 12.6 percent.[5]

Overall, there were serious challenges in the banking sector's outreach to the unbanked. According to the World Bank's Findex survey, only 23 percent of the adult population in Myanmar had access to formal financial services, while only 2 percent of the adult population had a debit card (compared to 26 percent in Indonesia and 55 percent in Thailand). Most of the population relied on informal channels such as payday lenders and pawnshops, which often charged exorbitant rates.

Prior to 2011, the supply of microfinance in Myanmar was the domain of international non-governmental organisations (NGOs) and the Myanmar Agriculture Development Bank (MADB). In 2011, the microfinance law was passed, which allowed local and foreign investors to establish privately owned MFIs in the country. In the years that followed, MFIs became increasingly prevalent in Myanmar, with 168 licensed MFIs operating in the country by 2017.[6] These institutions primarily offered small loans up to US$400.[7]

In 2015, according to the Asian Development Bank (ADB), the MFIs operating in Myanmar served an estimated 1.45 million clients (85 percent of which were women) and had a total loan portfolio of approximately US$200 million.[8] Most MFIs were based around high-population centres like Yangon, Mandalay, and Ayeyarwady. Remote regions had higher operating costs, given their lower population densities. The MFI sector included several prominent international NGOs and development organisations such as the UNDP, Accion, and World Vision. PACT Global Microfinance Fund (PGMF), the oldest and largest MFI in Myanmar, dominated the microfinance sector in the country, serving approximately 750,000 clients with US$125 million in loans. Despite PGMF's dominant position in the market, there was healthy competition and growth in other MFIs throughout the country.

The non-performing loan (NPL) rate for MFIs was extraordinarily low. Most loans were made to groups, rather than individuals, and given the strong social pressure to repay, most people paid back on time and in full. Cultural factors, such as people not wanting to be in debt in the future or be a burden on their families with debt when they died, also likely played a role.[9]

The MFI sector in Myanmar was following global trends in microfinance closely. These MFIs typically championed responsible financial principles such as corporate governance, risk management policies and procedures, and transparency at all levels, including investors, regulators, and clients.[10] Moreover, private sector MFIs tended to be well-capitalised and supported investment in technology, new products and services, and staff training and development.

Challenges faced by MFIs

Although the rise of private sector MFIs was helping to increase access to financial products and services to the poor in Myanmar, there were a number of challenges that needed to be addressed in order to significantly scale up and drive higher financial inclusion. One major constraint was that MFIs were not allowed to use voluntary deposits as a source of financing loans. To help ease this challenge, the Myanmar government changed the law in 2014 to allow foreign-owned MFIs to borrow from both local and foreign banks as long as they had the consent and approval of the Microfinance Supervisory Committee, Myanmar's regulatory body for the MFI sector.

According to numerous research studies, savings products, not loans, were found to have the greatest impact on reducing poverty. Despite this, a major constraint faced by MFIs was the strict limits placed on deposit-taking. Another major challenge was the lack of information sharing between MFIs or the lack of a credit bureau to check the creditworthiness of borrowers. Increased competition between MFIs had reduced the incentive to share information about clients, which indirectly encouraged borrowers to take out multiple loans from different MFIs, resulting in over-indebtedness.

FFMCL's key challenges

Although FFMCL was able to start successfully issuing loans within five months of obtaining its licence, the company experienced significant challenges during the process.

Low digital readiness

The lack of infrastructure was a major obstacle in setting up operations. Initially, the use of the Internet and mobile phones by the local population was extremely limited and very expensive. Since FFMCL wanted to adopt a primarily digital operation in order to be cost effective and efficient, having little to no access to reliable Internet services became a major issue.

To solve this problem, FFMCL decided to invest in and use very small aperture terminal (VSAT) satellite dishes to overcome the problem, VSAT was a significant investment, and obtaining the necessary approvals from the Ministry of Communication in Myanmar for the use of this technology proved challenging. The company also faced hurdles in obtaining approval for importing the VSAT dishes and other technical equipment such as biometric printers and thermal paper that were required to run the satellite dishes.

High digitisation costs

FFMCL's digitisation costs were more substantial compared to that of its peers and competitors who chose to employ manual processes. However, the investment in technology was a proven means to deliver better returns in the long run. As Myanmar opened up to new leadership, the country was beginning to experience a 'leapfrog' effect in investments related to cell phone tower infrastructure and broadband services. For instance, the cost of a SIM card dramatically dropped from approximately US$2,500 in 2013 to about US$1 in 2016.

Despite impressive improvements, access to broadband services in certain areas was still limited, and in some instances, the costs were still prohibitive. Nonetheless, broadband wireless allowed FFMCL to transition away from the more expensive VSAT to 4G for all of its operations by 2016, significantly bringing down the cost of running its core banking services.

Recruitment and staff training

Another major challenge that FFCML had to cope with was finding the right people to employ. Given the limited human resource development in Myanmar, it was difficult to hire individuals who had the right skill level for the different positions. Therefore, FFMCL invested in setting up a rigorous certification process for the people they hired. This process was very similar to the rigours imposed on those working in the banking sector, which had not been used before by MFIs. For instance, right from the time of inception, the company put in place a two-week orientation training programme, followed by work shadowing at branches with experienced staff. Furthermore, strong corporate governance standards, processes, and policies, including a know your customer/anti-money laundering (KYC/AML) as well as environmental and social framework and processes were implemented, which its staff needed to learn and adopt, even though this was not a requirement for MFIs.

The extended and comprehensive staff training allowed FFMCL to develop a high standard of employees, who were sought after by other financial institutions and MFIs in the country. Ultimately, FFMCL wanted to be the employer of choice among MFIs in Myanmar, providing its employees knowledge and training from both local experience and international practices.

Company culture

FFMCL's culture and mindset also contributed to the challenges in employee recruitment and retention. The company had created a unique incentive structure for loan officers, which was different from the traditional seniority-based system that was common in emerging markets. Essentially, FFMCL was interested in moving to a more performance-based incentive scheme, which resembled the developed economies of the United States and Europe.

Technology as enabler

FFH was a firm believer that technology was a key enabler in driving financial inclusion and had experienced the positive impact of digitisation in its operations in India. Based on this learning, FFMCL was set up to be fully digital in most of its operations from the very beginning. A digital solution provided not only cost efficiency but also the ability to scale up rapidly. When FFMCL launched for business, they pioneered the use of mobile tablets to replace paper forms and biometric devices for identification processes. Loan officers captured customer information on their devices to facilitate loan applications and subsequently loan repayments and loan take-up.

According to various people interviewed informally in Yangon, the time taken to get a loan approved by Myanmar's largest MFI, PGMF, was about one month. At FFMCL, it took only eight days, which included the time required for the training of group members and group recognition tests. Technology had made the process significantly more efficient, especially the KYC process, where clients need to provide proof of identity. FFMCL was the only MFI in Myanmar that used biometric identification systems for on-boarding their customers and for transaction authorisations. The digital approach had led to greater convenience and security for customers, who earlier had to provide their thumbprints as identification for every interaction. The risk of fraud was also mitigated and the speed of service delivery significantly enhanced.

As customer data was stored digitally, FFMCL was able to conduct customer analytics with ease. This enabled the company to understand the customers' needs accurately and accordingly provide appropriate products in affordable sizes. In 2017, 80 percent of MFI's borrowers stayed on to take succeeding loans, which reflected the relevant role the company played in their lives.

From an operational perspective, a cloud-based operating system was highly efficient since it allowed FFMCL to have minimal IT infrastructure in Myanmar and software updates could be run remotely and seamlessly without the need to take down servers for an extended period of time to install new patches or versions. This also overcame the difficulty of sourcing appropriately skilled technology staff to manage both the hardware infrastructure and software.

Technology with a human touch

While digital solutions clearly demonstrated its ability to achieve greater financial inclusion, having a completely digital process had been challenging for FFMCL, especially when it came to building customer trust in an environment where the customers were not technically savvy and had never used or experienced the benefits of digital solutions. Therefore, FFMCL strongly believed that the best approach was the use of 'technology with high touch.' In this regard, loan officers were still needed to develop relationships with customers, but the process of on-boarding a customer as well as collecting payments had been improved by using biometrics for identification and tablets by the loan officers to collect borrower information.

Looking ahead, the use of mobile wallets and digital payments could potentially make many consumer-facing banking processes even more efficient. In 2017, FFMCL started conducting pilot tests with several mobile wallets, such as Wave Money for loan repayments, which were still subject to Financial Regulatory Department (FRD) approval.

Sustainability and social impact—touching clients, improving their livelihood

In the entire lending process, FFMCL aimed to help its customers improve their lives by providing a social good. Specifically, every customer would undergo credit and finance education before the loan was disbursed. Group loan borrowers were required to undergo training to learn about the basics of loans, the meaning of a social guarantee, and the importance of timely repayments. By having this financial education, customers gained a better understanding of their responsibilities and were able to manage their resources better. In addition, for each group loan, there was a 'Group Recognition Test' session, where FFMCL verified that the group member had learned the basics before they disbursed the loans.

Focused on uplifting the lives of the grassroots community in Myanmar, FFMCL provided a range of unsecured loan products under a group lending model to assist micro-enterprises with working capital needs. Loans for specific purposes, such as agriculture, education, and healthcare, were also made available. FFMCL had also pioneered the disbursement of 'social' loans, such as solar lamp loans and eco-stove loans, to improve the living conditions of rural communities. For small business owners, especially in urban areas, the company extended working capital assistance through larger ticket loans under an individual lending model. Each borrower relationship was managed by a dedicated loan officer, who engaged with the borrower regularly. The loan officer would recommend products for the continuous improvement of the customer's enterprise.

More than 90 percent of the borrowers were women entrepreneurs who ran businesses to support their families. According to some women clients, the reason they borrowed money from FFMCL was because the MFI provided competitive rates and took care of them whenever there were any issues or crises. Moreover, the majority of these women reported that they were on their third or fourth loan from FFMCL after having repaid their initial loans.

FFMCL introduced two key products that provided a significant social impact for the borrowers: a savings account and insurance. All borrowers of a group loan were required to deposit 1,000 kyat (US$0.75) into a savings account when they took out a loan. The borrower deposited 300 kyat (US$0.23) in their savings account, part of which went towards their biweekly payment of interest and principal of the loan. Having a dedicated savings account allowed the borrowers to set aside funds in a financial institution, which they could use for healthcare or emergencies, paying for their children's education, or any other situation that might arise.

FFMCL also collaborated with an insurance provider to provide micro-insurance on the loans made to borrowers. Once the borrower took out a new loan, they were required to pay 1 percent of the loan amount for the micro-insurance. FFMCL, it seemed, was the first MFI to ensure that its customers had credit life insurance, which was helpful in times of uncertainty.

Furthermore, during times of crisis such as floods or fires, FFMCL was present to assist its customers, whether with immediate needs such as rice, beans and oil for cooking, and clean drinking water, as well as offering debt rescheduling where needed.

Next steps

The use of technology and the provision of innovative, customised loan products that truly met the needs of borrowers had enabled FFMCL to scale up quickly in Myanmar. Customers viewed FFMCL as part of their family, and they enjoyed the small, caring gestures from the company's employees, such as having their loans serviced at their homes, saving them time and money to travel to faraway branches.

Moreover, the customers felt that the loan officers really cared for them and always tried to find ways to help them. While technology provided more efficiency and transparency, allowing FFMCL to process more customised loans and increase the number of customers they were able to reach, the human touch and the drive to improve their clients' livelihood through financial education and social loans were equally important factors contributing to the company's success.

In 2017, FFMCL was evaluating its growth plans for the next five years, which were ambitious: the goal was to expand from 12 townships to 62, which would more than quadruple its reach. Mukherjee and the FFH team pondered how to achieve this growth. Should they open more branches? Or should they try something new, such as a 'hub and spoke' model, that is, using a central base while loan officers would travel from this location to villages on a daily basis? FFMCL wanted to maintain a positive social impact through financial empowerment. Yet, at the same time, it needed to ensure that it did not overextend loan growth and increase lending risk. Mukherjee and his team set their minds to work on hatching the next steps.

Notes

1 MMK17 billion as of May 2017, US$1 = MMK 1,324 as of February 2018, www.xe.com. Unless otherwise specified, all conversions have taken place at this rate through the case.

2 BBC News, "Myanmar Profile—Overview", 19 June 2015, www.bbc.com/news/world-asia-pacific-12990563.

3 Roland Berger, *Myanmar Banking Sector 2025: The Way Forward*, Munich: Roland Berger, September 2016.

4 Ibid.

5 James Seward, *Myanmar Access to Finance*, Washington, DC: World Bank, 2012.

6 VDB, www.vdb-loi.com/mlw/buying-shares-in-a-myanmar-microfinance-company.

7 Ibid.

8 Asian Development Bank, "Myanmar Microfinance Regulatory Benchmarking Survey", September 2016, www.mekongbiz.org/wp-content/uploads/2017/02/ADB-MBI-MF-Benchmarking-Survey-10-Oct16-final-proof-DG-AB.pdf.

9 Ibid.

10 Ibid.

3

YANGON BAKEHOUSE: A SOCIAL ENTERPRISE IN MYANMAR

Howard Thomas and Sheetal Mittal

Women play a particularly important role in social entrepreneurship, not only as entrepreneurs but also in championing women's empowerment in conservative Asian societies. In the case of 'Yangon Bakehouse: A Social Enterprise in Myanmar,' the enterprise strives to lend a hand to the underprivileged by taking on unskilled and uneducated women as culinary apprentices who would typically work for its restaurant and catering business upon completing their apprenticeship. As a commercial revenue-generating business, Yangon Bakehouse was able to break free from the restrictions imposed by donors on non-government organisations and did not have to depend on their generosity.

This case exemplifies how a social enterprise might descend into a financial crisis while trying to drive its mission of social inclusion. Given the absence of experienced management, the lack of legal recognition for social enterprises, and the low level of government support for small-scale entrepreneurs in Myanmar, it was challenging for Yangon Bakehouse to sustain growth despite initial success. To close the widening financial-social return gap, it needed to make use of innovative financing options, such as quasi-equity debt and direct public offering. However, the building of social capital through counselling support, soft skills education, and remuneration for the apprentices was equally important.

DOI: 10.4324/9781003203582-4

Yangon Bakehouse (YBH), a social enterprise based in Myanmar, was founded by Kelly Macdonald, a Canadian public health professional, and her three partners, one of whom was Daw Phyu Phyu Tin, a Burmese restaurateur. They conceived the idea of YBH in 2012 in their quest to provide both social skills and economic dignity to Burmese women. It was a critical time for Myanmar, as the country was just starting to embrace economic reforms. However, a large proportion of Burmese women were unskilled and uneducated and hence struggling to contribute to the emerging formal economy.

Eschewing the donor dependency model followed by NGOs, YBH applied commercial strategies to address the socio-economic development issues of disadvantaged women in Myanmar. It recruited minimally educated women who lacked a stable income into a seven-month-long multiskilling training programme that provided culinary skills for employability and life skills related to healthcare and financial decision-making. At the end of the training, the apprentices were helped in securing jobs in cafes, restaurants, and bakeries.

A key component of YBH's business model was its restaurant and catering business that served healthy Western cuisine through its cafés and online platform. The business served a dual purpose—it provided the apprentices on-the-job training in a practical setting and generated income to help sustain the training programme.

By end of 2017, YBH had managed to train and place 91 women. It ran two kiosks; one café; and a centralised kitchen, training centre, and office in a fourth location. However, the past five years had been riddled with obstacles such as the highly skewed real estate market in Myanmar requiring upfront deposit of one year's rent, restrictive loan policies of banks, and a lack of recognition of social enterprises by Myanmar laws. Also, being a social enterprise, and a successful one at that, YBH did not fit into the traditional norms and cultural values of charity pursued by Burmese companies, which preferred to target their corporate social responsibility (CSR) initiatives towards seemingly more destitute and hence worthier causes, such as orphanages, old-age homes, or monasteries.

Moreover, in the five years since YBH's inception, there had been significant cultural and economic changes in Myanmar that raised concerns about the long-term sustainability and relevance of its social enterprise model. Though the café generated revenue for the social enterprise, it came at the cost of high overheads. In addition, the enterprise needed to transition to local leadership and management, but given the tightrope it was on between being a NGO and a commercial business, it would require someone with a unique set of skills and experience. More importantly, going forward, should YBH focus on growing bigger or should it look inwards and build on what it was good at?

Social enterprise in Myanmar

The concept of social enterprise had emerged in Myanmar after Cyclone Nargis hit in 2008. The lack of large-scale international aid due to the military regime's restrictions had catalysed domestic players in funding and helping with disaster relief. Many entrepreneurs carried forward the momentum by channelling the resources generated from their businesses towards supporting social impact initiatives. In 2012, after its first elections in 20 years, Myanmar also looked to attract overseas investments for its for-profit businesses and social enterprises.

Although they were gaining popularity, social enterprises in Myanmar lacked a supportive regulatory environment, with no legal recognition and unfavourable taxation policies.[1] Lack of a legal status had led most social enterprises to register as NGOs, as associations (strictly focused on social or religious activities), or as private limited companies.[2] While registering as a private limited company was the easiest option, and many social enterprises, including YBH, did so, it attracted the same tax rate as that of a for-profit business. In addition, with Myanmar's financial system grossly underdeveloped, bank financing for small businesses was non-existent, creating large funding gaps ranging between US$50,000 and US$250,000. Furthermore, the typically small management teams running such ventures were overworked, while the available workforce in the country woefully lacked the requisite skills. Such barriers severely limited a social enterprise's potential to grow and scale up operations.[3]

Status of women in Myanmar

In 2013, women made up more than half the population, 51.8 percent, in Myanmar, but less than 25 percent were part of the nation's work force.[4] Gender gaps in employment were high across all states of the country and across all age groups.[5] One-fifth of women above the age of 25 had not completed primary education. Even women who possessed higher educational qualifications had lower labour participation and experienced a 30 percent wage disparity compared to men.[6] Despite being legally entitled to equal rights and status in society, Burmese women had been historically subjected to discrimination and abuse.[7] Few had knowledge of their rights. Gender-based violence strongly undermined women's capacities and contributed to their poor sexual and reproductive health. Exclusionary practices also limited their ability to leave abusive relationships, be financially independent, and achieve socio-economic dignity.

Yangon Bakehouse

Conceptualising the business model

Having worked in the development sector since 1995, Macdonald believed that the donor-dependent model of NGOs not only curtailed their freedom to operate but also led them to becoming unsustainable in the longer run. Thus, in 2012, she decided to set up a self-sustaining enterprise that would have a revenue-generating business unit that supported its social mission.

Macdonald believed that economically empowering socially disadvantaged women would help them to make better choices not only for themselves but also for their families and the community's health and welfare. Unskilled women with low levels of education made up a huge segment of the population that had traditionally not been economically engaged. Many earned petty amounts on a day-to-day basis by selling snacks, some were sex workers who wanted to leave the trade, and some just fell into poverty due to the lack of any social safety net. Though Myanmar's economy and the work force had started to change since 2012, the rapidly growing industry primarily looked for people who were educated.

Macdonald also identified an opportunity on the business side. In 2012, due to Myanmar's near lockdown under military rule, the people lacked exposure to healthy, fresh, and home-style Western food options. However, as the country opened up, Macdonald felt that the demand for these options was bound to go up with an increasing influx of foreigners and the growing diaspora that had started to return to Yangon. To her, this market gap represented an attractive business opportunity.

Macdonald identified two sets of skills that YBH needed to inculcate among the targeted women: culinary and baking skills to make them job ready and the social skills to instil in them self-confidence to be able to find a job, negotiate, take different decisions, and take responsibility for those decisions. Technical training was just half the battle towards ensuring sustainable financial inclusion of these women. The soft skills were imperative but could only be imparted if the women were in good health and aware of their rights. Hence, they also needed to be educated about their reproductive health status (contraceptive care and methods), nutrition needs for overall wellbeing, and their role and rights in the family and society.

YBH incorporated all these elements in its programme, but with just four people at the helm, it did not have the ability to provide complete training. Hence, it collaborated with other NGOs operating in Yangon that had the expertise and outsourced different modules of the programme to them. For example, CARE Myanmar carried out CEDAW[8] training; YWCA conducted the module on saving strategies and planning, communication, and decision-making skills; Shwe Hnin Si Foundation provided reproductive cancer awareness and training on conducting self-tests; Marie Stopes International ran a programme on contraceptive and sexual disease knowledge; and Akhaya helped the trainees develop a deeper understanding of their own sexuality.

YBH also reached out to private-sector players like the banks. Between 2014 and 2017, there was a shift in the way the banking industry was looked upon in Myanmar, and ATM machines mushroomed in the country. Prior to that, the Burmese generally did not believe in putting their money in banks. They had little knowledge about the banking industry and did not trust the system. To overcome this, YBH collaborated with Cooperative Bank to educate women about the concept of savings and how a bank could help in the process. Use of bank accounts was a big part of the YBH's social mission, as it compelled the women to take ownership of their income and make financial decisions based on a paycheck every month instead of just a day's income earned sporadically as part of the informal economy. These seemingly simple skills of monthly financial planning were considerably important for entry into the formal economy.

Another highlight of YBH's model was that all apprentices were paid monthly during the training period to compensate them for what they could have possibly earned during those months. With financial inclusion as YBH's primary goal, not doing so would have defeated its very purpose. However, this escalated the costs, as the start-up had to pay salaries to both trainers and trainees.

The seed capital for the start-up was raised publicly through Indiegogo, a crowdfunding site. The founders also invested their personal funds in the social enterprise.

Setting up

In December 2012, YBH enrolled its first batch of six women apprentices through its partner NGOs. The training programme, which was initially held at the partners' homes, was moved to YBH's first café that opened three months later. By the end of the year, it moved to a separate office space.

The demand for YBH's food items grew rapidly, and soon the café was operating seven days a week. The café largely relied on locally sourced ingredients, keeping the food healthy and fresh. It also started to stock produce from small local producers who were located in remote regions, had limited access to the consumer market, and did not know how to market and sell their products. The producers had to comply with YBH's quality norms and packaging specifications if they wanted their products stocked in the café.

Expansion

By 2014, the demand for YBH products had multiplied and was soon beyond the service capacity of its one and only café. Ooredoo, one of the big telecom companies that had recently entered Myanmar, provided YBH with a space to set up its staff canteen at no rental cost. This CSR initiative by Ooredoo enabled YBH to have a second space free for close to two years. When Ooredoo's office moved to another location in 2015, YBH decided to open a second café on the premises, in addition to building a central kitchen at a third location. To build the kitchen, YBH took a low-interest loan from an overseas religious community that wanted to support the enterprise.

The news about YBH's food spread through word of mouth. In 2014, YBH expanded into food catering services due to the growing demand for orders for special events. Embassies and NGOs, in particular, were driven to order through YBH, as it contributed to the local community, and hence they preferred to use their entertainment budget on a social enterprise rather than a commercial business. By 2017, the catering business grew to 25 percent of YBH's total revenues, contributing significantly to the venture's profitability and providing another source of income generation within the same fixed overhead costs.

YBH also offered home delivery services (charging a delivery fee of one-way taxi fare) for orders received on phone or through its website. It also partnered with 'door to door,' an online retail company that used bicycles to deliver orders received on its portal. While the company charged a high price for delivery, online ordering was a growing part of YBH's business (3–5 percent of total revenues).

Competition

When YBH started out in 2012–13, it hardly faced any competition. However, by 2015, as Myanmar's economy opened up, a growing demand for Western products led to an increasing presence of Western-style eating-places. Macdonald felt that the competition was good for YBH, as it prompted a regular review of its products in line with the evolving needs of the customers, a skill that was essential in achieving sustainability.

> *Other cafes kept us on our toes. We learnt how not to act as a typical NGO in order to attract enough customers, and instead ran our business successfully.*

More importantly, the competition played a vital role in helping YBH meet one of its primary goals—to get the trained apprentices employed in the industry. According to Macdonald, "First and foremost we are a training programme working towards the financial inclusion of our women." With the opening of similar cafes and restaurants, job opportunities grew and finding placement for the apprentices became easier.

Growing pains

One of the initial problems faced by YBH was to retain the recruited candidates over the length of the training period. It suffered from an average dropout rate of 25 percent. Given the nature of work at the bake house, trainees had to work eight-hour shifts that either started at 5:00 am or finished at 7:00 pm in the evening. These hours clashed with the time required for traditional roles that the women played in their households. In addition, in some instances, because the women brought home a fatter paycheck than the males in their household, it created disharmony in the patriarchal society. Hence, the family members disapproved and pressured the women to leave mid-way through. Another concern was the inability of some women to hold onto their jobs after graduating from YBH.

With time, the recruitment process evolved, and YBH learnt to better match the candidate profile and needs with the enterprise's objectives. It also engaged a social protection support person to provide the apprentices with counselling support, through either one-on-one or peer group sessions. Consequently, the dropout rate came down to 15 percent.

By 2017, the operating costs of running two cafés escalated, with the real estate market in Yangon sharply increasing. Besides high rentals, an entire year's rent was required to be paid upfront. In addition, with time, the kitchen equipment warranted frequent maintenance, repair, and replacement. Additionally, with YBH committed to bringing in local management to run the organisation, it meant higher costs, as salaries would need to be paid, unlike Macdonald and her partners who worked pro bono (they took no salaries, and all profits were reinvested in the bake house).

With government policies biased towards large organisations, bank loans were not available for small entrepreneurs like YBH. Alternative sources of funding through grants and donations also proved an uphill task despite the country's pro-charity Buddhist culture and a growing CSR movement with many local companies aligning with the United Nations Global Compact.[9] Having had to register as a commercial business, YBH was not favoured by either the government or private-sector companies for grants or CSR initiatives. Moreover, as a business entity, not only was YBH subject to the commercial tax rate, but the donations received were not eligible for tax benefits.

Increasing expenses and inaccessibility of capital severely limited YBH's ability to sustain growth and develop future plans. In March 2017, facing another hike in rental cost, it had to close down its second café and put on hold its plans of expanding the catering business.

As a social enterprise striving to be financially self sustaining, YBH struggled at both ends—it had to not only curtail its growth by limiting itself to just one café and two kiosks but also had to scale down the intake of the number of apprentices for training.

New strategies

Financial restructuring

To close the financial-social return gap, Yangon Bakehouse would need to make use of a myriad of financing options available through restructuring its business model. According to Bugg-Levine, Kogut, and Kulatilaka (2012), like commercial businesses, a social enterprise can also pose different risks and returns to different investors instead of delivering a standard mix of social benefits and financial revenues.[10] It needed to consider that charitable donations are also a form of investment just like debt and equity and have investors that need to be catered to. The understanding that (1) there are three types of financing instruments: charity, debt, and equity; (2) they offer different levels of risks and types of returns; and (3) they can be bundled in different proportions according to the available investor pool has led to the development of many innovative solutions to broaden social enterprises' access to funds (refer to Table 3.1 for the characteristics of each instrument).

YBH could use any of the following financing options.

Donor and equity hybrid model[11]

Conventional businesses can raise capital as a mix of equity and debt, whereby the equity partners seek riskier and higher returns and the debt investors seek low but predictable returns. Similarly, a social enterprise can also seek capital from two different types of investors: donors or social impact investors who want to see their money generate social benefits but do not want

Table 3.1 Types of Financing for Social Enterprises

Types	*Payment Structure*	*Claim on Assets*	*Types of Return*
Charitable	None	None	Social good
Equity	Variable	Residual	High financial risk and return
Debt	Fixed	Fixed	Low risk and return

Source: Adapted from Bugg-Levine, Antony, Bruce Kogut, and Nalin Kulatilaka. "A new approach to funding social enterprises." Harvard Business Review, Vol.90 Issue: 1/2, 2012: pp. 118–123.

their money back, and financial investors who are looking for a predictable and reasonably healthy rate of return on their investment.

The hybrid model can be illustrated with an example. Say YBH needs to raise US$200,000. If it can generate revenue of the order of US$10,000 a year through its restaurant business, this would mean an annual return of 5 percent on the investment of US$200,000. This may be too low a return to attract equity investors, while the total capital required may be too large an amount to raise only through donations. Therefore, YBH can split the capital into two portions such that it raises US$100,000 through donations and the rest through financial investors. Then it can offer an attractive 10 percent return on the US$100,000 to financial investors. This is a win-win solution for all three stakeholders: YBH is able to raise the funding, the donor needs to donate only half the funds (freeing the remaining capital for other social causes), and the equity investor earns a better return on investment.

Quasi-equity debt[12]

Quasi-equity debt is essentially a debt instrument, but its returns are linked to the financial performance of the social enterprise. It offers a medium-rate financial risk and return (typically higher than debt but lower than equity). A social fund may comprise a number of social enterprises using a quasi-equity debt format, and social investors may invest in the fund as equity.

The instrument can allow YBH to frame the loan agreement such that it would incentivise the YBH management to operate the enterprise efficiently without giving any ownership rights to the investor (unlike in the case of equity investment).

Direct-public offering/democratic finance[13]

A direct-public offering (DPO) allows social enterprises to seek funds directly from the public (a large number of individuals or a community of interest) in a flexible manner through equity shares, debt financing, revenue shares, crowd funding, or any other such instrument. Furthermore, investors are not subjected to any minimum asset requirements and do not need the services of an investment bank to buy the instrument.

While DPOs can be quite successful in sourcing funds from the local community, YBH would need to ascertain whether they are allowed in Myanmar and what the administrative regulations are. For example, per the Myanmar Investment Act of 2017, if even one share is foreign owned, the entire venture is treated as a foreign enterprise and is subject to restrictions on capital flows.

Integrated capital[14]

Similar to the hybrid model, integrated capital is a coordinated mix of a wide range of different forms of capital such as equity, loans, gifts, grants, and loan guarantees. Inclusion of funds that warrant little or no returns mitigates the cost of capital significantly and is particularly suitable for enterprises like YBH that have a successful business model but need low-cost funding to be able to grow and sustain their operations. Also, by allowing local investors and the public to participate, integrated capital (and DPOs) helps in creating a community commitment to the enterprise's success.

Pooling[15]

This allows loan portfolios from many micro-lenders to be assembled together and bundled into different categories with varied risks and returns for different types of investors.

Loan guarantees[16]

Reputable foundations issue loan guarantees to the social enterprises they support. This enables an enterprise to raise stable funding.

Program-related investments[17]

Program-related investment (PRI) funders, such as foundations, invest in social enterprise projects that are related to their mission. They tend to maintain their principal, are open to earning a low rate of return, and have greater risk tolerance than conventional investors.

Listed retail charity bond[18]

This is a bond for charities that is listed on a stock exchange and helps in raising unsecured debt from a number of individuals and institutions. It offers a low rate of return and is usually paid back over 12 years but can be for a shorter period. Being listed allows investors to buy and sell individual bonds quickly and at their convenience. However, this instrument is meant only for registered charities and will not be applicable to YBH, as it is registered as a 'for-profit' business in Myanmar.

It is important to note that despite the innovative financial solutions, there remains one major concern for prospective investors: the inability to track tangibly the impact of their money in a social enterprise. While there are efforts afoot to bring criteria, precision, and transparency to the social outcomes of social enterprises, it remains a highly intricate and complex task. The mechanisms for evaluating social risks and returns are still in a nascent stage of development in many markets, including Myanmar, thus making it difficult for enterprises like YBH to attract stable funding. Thus, YBH must demonstrate value and accountability to potential investors by adopting transparent accounting and reporting measures and providing real-time access to its operations and financial performance.

Collaborative value creation

Another factor that plays a crucial role in enabling the sustainable operations of social enterprises is collaborative value creation by working with like-minded organisations. Due to their shared social vision, these social impact partnerships tend to be far more rewarding and effective than purely financial ones based on rate on investment. YBH had an active partnership with many NGOs and a few private-sector players that supported the enterprise in providing different modules of the training programme to its apprentices. However, as a social enterprise, it has the potential to have a much wider interface with multilateral lending institutions and CSR efforts of multinational corporations. For example, the World Bank offers a massive platform to connect with social impact investors who have the resources to support social visions. It also runs a programme called 'development marketplace' to promote small-scale social enterprises by providing them with the much needed seed money. Similarly, foundations such as Ashoka or Schwab not only help by providing seed capital but also help by making crucial support networks accessible.[19]

Large corporations with their CSR initiatives are also effective and resourceful partners providing managerial knowledge, skills, and capabilities, in addition to corporate funding. Teaming up with a global corporation in its CSR efforts may help YBH overcome the problems it faced in finding suitable local managerial resources, as well as managing the hiring costs. Many experts in the domain suggest that ventures like YBH can be the crucial link between the needs of humanity and the social responsibility of corporates, helping in channelising the resources and expertise of corporates to create social impact.[20]

However, to be associated with global platforms sponsored by organisations like the World Bank, rope in large corporations as its partners, or attract social impact investors, YBH should be able to instil trust among its potential stakeholders. To that end, it needs to develop a strong 'not-for-profit' brand, just like for-profit businesses, that would help it connect, gain resources, and establish long-term partnerships. Branding becomes even more important for a social enterprise than a commercial venture, as the former have more intangible goals that are complex to achieve and difficult to measure. Nevertheless, developing a brand also requires resources, and this is one of the key challenges faced by enterprises like YBH.

Social entrepreneurship is an evolving space, and organisations like YBH need to build wider networks, seek new collaborations, and adopt innovative financial solutions to ensure long-term sustainability. On the other hand, there is a growing dilemma in the social sector about what should be more important—the financial means or the social goals? Policy makers the world over are not always consistent or enlightened on the merits of each of these goals. Does the focus on one lead to less than optimal results for the other?

Notes

1 Michael Standaert, "A Social Investment Ecosystem Emerges in Vietnam, Cambodia and Myanmar", *Impact Alpha*, 12 June 2017, https://news.

impactalpha.com/a-social-investment-ecosystem-emerges-in-vietnam-cambodia-and-myanmar-4d9138abofff.

2 British Council, *Social Enterprise Landscape in Myanmar*, British Council, 2013, https://iixglobal.com/wp-content/uploads/2013/09/2013_SE-Landscape-in-Myanmar_British-Council.compressed.pdf.

3 Ibid.

4 MIMU, "The 2014 Myanmar Population and Housing Census", http://themimu.info/census-data.

5 UNFPA, "The 2014 Myanmar Population and Housing Census: Thematic Report on Gender Dimensions", August 2017, http://themimu.info/sites/themimu.info/files/documents/Report_Thematic_Report_on_Gender_Dimensions_-_Census_Report_4-J_DOP_Aug2017_ENG.pdf.

6 Ibid.

7 Alliance for Gender Inclusion in the Peace Process, "Gender Inequality in Myanmar", www.agipp.org/en/gender-inequality-myanmar.

8 The Convention on the Elimination of all Forms of Discrimination against Women.

9 A strategic policy initiative for businesses to be committed to ten universally accepted principles in the areas of human rights, labour, environment and anti-corruption. For more information, please refer to www.unglobalcompact.org/.

10 Anthony Bugg-Levine, Bruce Kogut, and Nalin Kulatilaka, "A New Approach to Funding Social Enterprises", *Harvard Business Review*, 90(1/2) (2012): 118–123.

11 Ibid.

12 Ibid.

13 Don Shaffer, "Growth Financing for Social Enterprises: 5 Options and How to Make Them Work for You", *Triple Pundit*, 18 February 2015, www.triplepundit.com/2015/02/growth-financing-social-enterprises-5-options-make-work/.

14 Ibid.

15 Anthony Bugg-Levine, Antony, Bruce Kogut, and Nalin Kulatilaka, "A New Approach to Funding Social Enterprises", *Harvard Business Review*, 90(1/2) (2012): 118–123.

16 Ibid.

17 Impact Ventures, "Financing Social Enterprise Growth", E3M, www.impactventuresuk.com/wp-content/uploads/2015/06/E3M_Financing-Growth_May-2015.pdf.

18 Ibid.

19 Christian Seelos and Johanna Mair, "Social Entrepreneurship: Creating New Business Models to Serve the Poor", *Business Horizons*, 48(3) (2005): 241–246.

20 Ibid.

4

SURECASH: PROMOTING FINANCIAL INCLUSION IN BANGLADESH

Aurobindo Ghosh and Lipika Bhattacharya

In this chapter, we describe the journey of SureCash, a mobile financial service (MFS) provider in Dhaka, Bangladesh, operating in an oligopolistic market dominated by two large players. SureCash had used a niche strategy to grow in the market by associating itself with government-led projects like the Primary Education Stipend Program (PESP), which was designed to increase educational participation, enrolment, and attendance of primary school children from low-income families in the country. The project distributed stipends to mothers of students every quarter in the form of cash payments. SureCash faced many difficulties in digitising the PESP initiative due to challenges posed by large amounts of physical data and disbursal of funds in remote areas. However, there was significant value in executing the program, as it tried to promote financial inclusion for rural women—a section of the demographic who were less likely to have access to formal financial services. The key dilemma is whether SureCash can continue to keep women motivated to use their accounts regularly in the future.

The case tries to encapsulate important elements of an MFS market in a developing economy and describes some of the unique characteristics and risks of an oligopoly market. It also highlights some of the social and behavioural facets of financial inclusion in the context of MFS and explains the primary risks associated with the market from the customer and provider perspectives.

DOI: 10.4324/9781003203582-5

In December 2017, Matteo Chiampo, an advisor for SureCash, a mobile financial services provider in Bangladesh, wondered if his company had at last found the right strategy to operate in the MFS market. SureCash had collaborated with a state-owned commercial bank to launch a mobile banking service to disburse primary education stipends to low-income mothers of primary school students in the country. Banking regulations in Bangladesh required MFS providers to collaborate with state-owned banks, thereby ensuring that they were under the supervision of the Bangladesh Bank (BB), the banking regulatory authority in the country.

Launched by the government of Bangladesh in 2002, the Primary Education Stipend Project was designed to increase educational participation, enrolment, and attendance of primary school children from low-income families in the country. The project distributed a stipend to mothers of students every quarter in the form of cash payments. By 2016, the PESP initiative had run into challenges, realising that manual cash stipend disbursement was cumbersome and onerous, and had started to review possible digital options. SureCash had seized the opportunity to facilitate digitisation of the PESP project.

By early 2017, SureCash had successfully transitioned PESP to a digital platform and opened accounts for 10 million women, transferring stipend funds for 13 million students. The company's customer base had increased overnight by around 300%. However, despite the success, the CEO of SureCash, Shahadat Khan, was sceptical of the growth opportunities of his relatively small company.

The MFS sector in Bangladesh was essentially an oligopoly dominated by two large players: bKash, which held more than half of the market share, and Dutch Bangla Bank Limited (DBBL), which owned about one-sixth of the subscribers' market share. Khan had asked Chiampo to consider the kind of growth strategy a small player like SureCash could implement in such a market. The objective was to expand the firm's existing niche market strategy to target additional customer segments that had remained financially excluded despite the proliferation of MFS solutions in the market.

Role of MFS in promoting financial inclusion

SureCash had created its niche market strategy after assessing the impact of MFS services in rural communities in Bangladesh. The firm had noted that a critical benefit of financial inclusion was the domino effect it could have in driving the rural economy and promoting social inclusion. Financial inclusion in rural societies created more empowered communities by providing access to accounts, savings, and payment systems. This, in turn, promoted ensuing investment within the community, creating jobs and boosting income levels. The significance of MFS in promoting financial inclusion, reducing poverty, and achieving inclusive growth has been discussed at length in extant literature.[1] Access to MFS services provided multi-faceted advantages, the majority of which could be categorised into two broad categories of economic and social goals. It not only fostered GDP growth, jobs, and rural entrepreneurship but also promoted social inclusion and integrated the socially excluded population into all domains of society (refer to Figure 4.1).

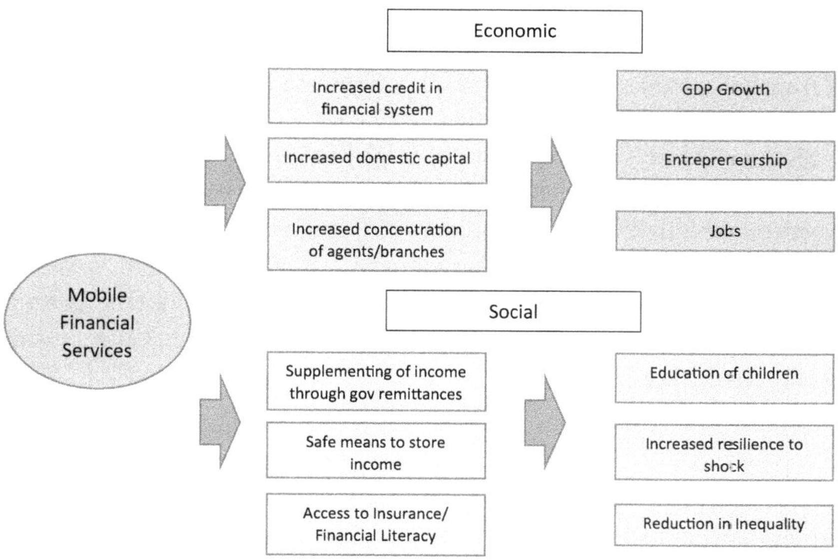

Figure 4.1 Socio-Economic Impact of MFS

Source: The Boston Consulting Group, The Socio-Economic Impact of Mobile Financial Services, Analysis of Pakistan, Bangladesh, India, Serbia and Malaysia, April 2011, www.telenor.com/wp-content/uploads/2012/03/The-Socio-Economic-Impact-of-Mobile-Financial-Services-BCG-Telenor-Group-2011.pdf.

The MFS market in Bangladesh

MFS in Bangladesh had been established as part of the government's regulatory reforms, which allowed financial service providers to operate in the country in partnership with a locally registered bank. These reforms were introduced in early 2011, following which the two companies DBBL and bKash had entered the market almost immediately.

The market conditions at the time had worked to the advantage of the two first movers. Mobile reseller outlets were facing challenging times, as margins on reselling airtime had fallen dramatically in 2012. Thus, when bKash and DBBL entered the market, mobile airtime reseller outlets jumped at the opportunity to become MFS agents, as it provided them some extra revenue from agency fees and also increased customer traffic to their outlets. Within the first two years of operation, bKash had converted the customers of nearly all mobile network operators in the country. By 2015, bKash had become the clear market leader, with 58 percent of the market share.[2] By October 2016, the company accounted for 89 percent of the total MFS transactions, with the second market leader, DBBL, accounting for another 10 percent. In terms of transaction value, bKash was the clear frontrunner, accounting for about 76 percent of the amount transacted.[3]

Having one or two large dominant players in the market had several drawbacks for smaller MFS players like SureCash. These included bleaker prospects for building large agent networks, less control on transaction fees, and more challenging brand management. In addition, there were also known market risks like local agents allowing registration of fake accounts without ensuring proper verification and daily operational challenges related to interoperability.[4]

Tackling an oligopolistic market

Rather than competing directly with its competitors, SureCash used a niche strategy to engage in the MFS market. The firm stumbled upon the specialised fee collection need of educational institutions and introduced solutions to meet this unmet market need. Most educational institutions in the country were at the time still maintaining piles of physical ledger books to keep track of student fees and payments, which was proving increasingly inconvenient. With the adoption of the SureCash digital mobile payment system, the student fee collection process became simpler and more efficient with convenient report generation, tracking, and reminders. Some institutions had further customised the automated platform and added solution features to roll out vaccination service initiatives, fingerprint identification technology for hostel students, and library automation solutions. By 2016, more than 200 educational institutions were collecting semester and monthly tuition fees using the SureCash educational fee collection platform.

Surecash also started promoting its platform to organisations for salary disbursements. Firms like Grameen Trust, Integrated Development Foundation, Grameen Shakti, and FoodPanda started disbursing salaries, transport allowances, and vendor payments using the platform. Some rural banks also began venturing into disbursing loans and collecting payments using SureCash. In 2016, Grameen Bank signed a memorandum of understanding to use the SureCash mobile payment platform for its operations. Through this partnership, Grameen Bank members were able to use SureCash mobile banking to receive loans and make instalment payments using their mobile phones. This proved a great opportunity to introduce the benefits of MFS to around 8.8 million Grameen Bank members, covering 97 percent of villages in Bangladesh. Later that year, other government agencies, such as the Water Supply and Sewage Authority and Bangladesh West Zone Power Distribution Board, began collaborating with SureCash to collect utility bill payments from their consumers.

In 2017, SureCash collaborated with Rupali Bank to take over the massive task of digitisation of the government-led PESP initiative. The aim of the PESP stipend was to cover the expenses of primary school education for students of low-income families. SureCash took on the responsibility of disbursing education stipends to the mothers of 13 million students and opened one mobile banking account for each mother so that they could receive the stipends directly into their accounts/mobile wallets. They could withdraw the stipend money from any Rupali Bank SureCash agent outlet, use it to make payments, or save it for the future.

As each mother listed in the programme had a bank account opened in her name, this also helped expedite financial inclusion of women and build women's empowerment. However, implementing a digitised disbursement method for the program was not an easy feat. PESP had been executed manually so far, using paperwork as a method of recording beneficiary sign-up and disbursement. SureCash soon realised that scanning physical paper forms on such an immense scale was a daunting task. There were about 10 million stipend recipients and several forms for each recipient. Piling up all these paper forms would have created an 8.5-km-tall tower of paper. Additionally, each form needed to be validated, scanned, and digitised. The firm also had to interact with different channels, including mobile network operators, government officials, and individual school personnel, which was a huge operational responsibility.

Despite the daunting challenge, SureCash decided that this was an opportunity. As a technology-oriented company, SureCash tapped what it was best at doing—that is, finding and building technology-based solutions to cope with the challenges. Instead of relying on commercial software, it leveraged its in-house technical skills to create a software development kit (SDK) and customise a third-party optical character recognition (OCR) solution.[5] The custom application could display the scanned image of the form and the corresponding recognised text side by side. This made the operator's checking process easier. The firm also added a flagging feature to indicate the level of recognition confidence using a colour-coded background, which guided the human operator's attention to the least accurate fields, thus helping speed up the human validation process. To digitise PESP within a short timeframe (a few months), the company installed 45 high-speed scanners capable of processing 60 pages per minute and set up a form processing centre with 240 staff.

Additionally, SureCash collaborated with Teletalk, a state-owned telecom provider, for the program. As part of the collaboration, Teletalk distributed a free SIM card with 20 BDT (US$0.24)[6] free talk time and 1 GB of data per month to all stipend recipients.[7]

The government of Bangladesh also had further objectives and aspirations from the digitised PESP program. Providing mobile phones to rural women could help them launch healthcare initiatives targeted towards these women. Moreover, access to the transaction information of these recipients could help them determine if there were potential candidates that they could target for imparting training for self-employment initiatives. The government also had plans to introduce a savings scheme for recipients to promote savings habits among rural women and lay a strong foundation of economic growth in the process.[8]

Niche market strategy

SureCash had been able to leverage a niche market strategy to its business advantage by associating with government projects and educational institutions. This strategy encompassed three factors: the existence of sufficient market demand in the niche, a low degree of competition in the niche, and a high income potential in the niche (refer to Figure 4.2).[9]

The niche strategy primarily targeted women and students. In Bangladesh, women had much lower access to mobile phones and mobile financial accounts as compared to men. In 2017, the percentage of women with mobile financial accounts was 36 percent compared to 65 percent for men, and mobile phone penetration was 47 percent compared to 76 percent for men.[10] Hence, there was substantial market potential for innovative services targeted towards women. Besides, the two leading market players were largely focused on P2P transfers, and the rural women customer segment constituted a low degree of competition.

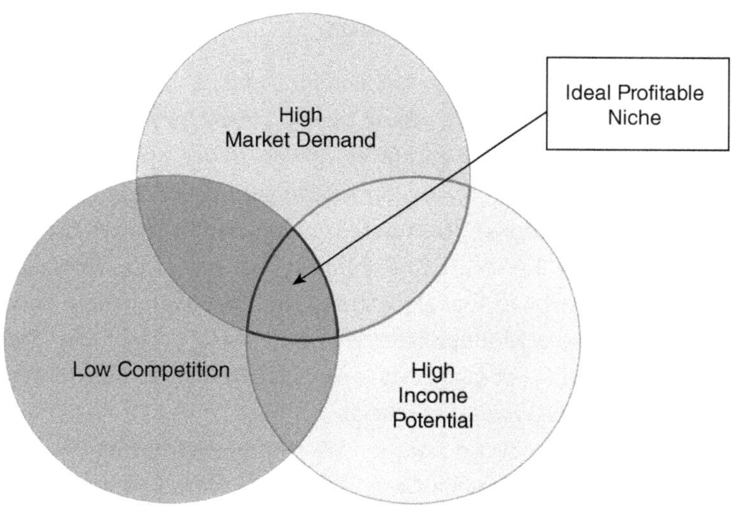

Figure 4.2 Niche Market Strategy

Source: Reproduced from Niche Marketing, Explore the Strategy of Niche Marketing, the Ideal Niche.

The road ahead

SureCash had been able to target rural women and effectively implement a niche strategy to operate in an oligopolistic market. But digital disruption had begun to change the scope of markets across geographies. For instance, while smartphone penetration within rural Bangladesh was still low, in neighbouring India, smartphones had quickly gained popularity over basic mobile phones even within the poorer sections of society. The entry of smartphones into the MFS market meant a host of new service possibilities for mobile banking users. What remained to be seen was whether SureCash could continue to drive growth by collaborating with other government initiatives such as PESP.

Could SureCash keep mothers engaged on its MFS platform over the long run? Could it tap on the opportunity that arose from the adoption of smartphones to establish itself as the front-runner of emerging technology solutions in the Bangladesh MFS market? What other market segments could the firm explore to expand its niche market?

Notes

1 The World Bank, *Inclusive Innovations, Mobile Money—Transforming Financial Inclusion*, World Bank, 2014, https://www.innovationpolicyplatform.org/www.innovationpolicyplatform.org/system/files/01%20Finance_BMI_Mobile%20%20Money-Merged-jsCLEAN_0_0/index.pdf.

2 Greg Chen and Stephen Rasmussen, *bKash Bangladesh: A Fast Start for Mobile Financial Services*, CGAP Publications, July 2014, www.cgap.org/web-publication/bkash-bangladesh-fast-start-mobile-financial-services.

3 "Mobile Money a Monopolistic Market: Official", *The Daily Star*, Star Business Report, 9 February 2017, www.thedailystar.net/business/mobile-money-monopolistic-market-official.

4 International Finance Corporation, *Achieving Interoperability in Mobile Financial Services*, Tanzania Case Study, 2015, https://www.ifc.org/wps/wcm/connect/d16ceebb-1853-4a2a-89f3-52985f8e5134/IFC+Tanzania+Interoperability+Case+Study.pdf?MOD=AJPERES&CVID=lA4tZDN.

5 ABBYY, "ABBY Mobile OCR Engine", www.abbyy.com/en-apac/mobile-ocr/.

6 BDT 1 = US$0.24, www.xe.com.

7 Engender Health, "Mayer Hashi", www.engenderhealth.org/our-work/major-projects/mayer-hashi-ii/.

8 Jannatul Islam, "Digital Payments for Cashless Society", *Daily Sun*, 31 July 2017.

9 Eli Noy, "Niche Strategy: Merging Economic and Marketing Theories with Population Ecology Arguments", *Journal of Strategic Marketing*, 18 (2010): 77–86.

10 Joep Roest, *Global Findex: Behind the Numbers on Bangladesh*, CGAP Publications, 2017, https://www.cgap.org/blog/2017-global-findex-behind-numbers-bangladesh#:~:text=At%2029%20percentage%20points%2C%20it,gender%20gaps%20in%20the%20world.&text=Overall%2C%20Findex%20shows%20that%2065,percent%20of%20women%20have%20accounts.

5

VERIOWN: CONNECTING THE INVISIBLE WOMAN IN INDIA

Howard Thomas and Sheetal Mittal

In the face of a multitude of difficulties under less-than-ideal conditions, social enterprises demonstrate their ability to think out of the box. In the case study of 'Veriown: Connecting the Invisible Woman in India,' the founder was deeply moved by a video of a young woman working under poor lighting conditions. This drove him to set up Veriown with the objective to provide solar energy, a safer and cleaner alternative to kerosene, a polluting and harmful fuel commonly used in India. He also observed that poverty-stricken rural Indians lacked access to connectivity and finance, thus prompting him to partner with telecom provider Vodafone and non-banking financial company DMI to package internet and micro-loan services with Veriown's core offering of solar-powered electricity.

This case highlights the significance of the concepts of value creation and value delivery for a social enterprise. It introduces a unique business model that innovatively bundles three services into one, along with a 'pay-as-you-consume' service. To create value, Veriown developed an efficient and cost-effective value chain by leveraging existing infrastructure, collaborating with the local community, and adopting a do-it-yourself model. In addition, it maximised value delivery by establishing an efficient last-mile distribution network through its partnership with Vodafone and DMI.

DOI: 10.4324/9781003203582-6

In August 2018, Steve Johanns, founder of Veriown Global, an Internet-connected solar energy provider, was just two months away from the launch of Veriown's platform in its first market—India. The success of its product in Uttar Pradesh and Bihar, the two largest and most underdeveloped states of the country, was crucial for the company to establish the viability of Veriown's business model, its scalability within India, and expansion into sub-Saharan Africa.

Established in 2016, Veriown's primary objective was to bridge the infrastructural gap in energy that existed in developing countries by providing a safer and cleaner alternative to kerosene, a non-renewable fossil fuel that was detrimental to health and the environment. Besides energy, Veriown aimed to facilitate digital connectivity and access to financial services to help enable socioeconomic development and financial inclusion of the impoverished rural communities.

Empowered by a strong team, and supported by global partners, Veriown had developed an advanced solar energy-based solution that brought electricity, the Internet, and microfinance services together on the same platform and followed the 'pay-to-consume' model that consumers at the bottom of the pyramid (BoP) preferred. It had also partnered with local companies with expertise in distribution and installation of solar energy solutions in rural India for on-ground support during the launch.

However, despite all the planning, Johanns was concerned about the operational capability of Veriown in meeting the high consumer demand of the market. He wondered if its service levels would be able to keep up with the demand and effectively resolve any issues as and when they appeared. In addition, would the company be able to scale up soon after the launch, if required?

Energy poverty

In 2017, about 1.2 billion people across the world did not have access to an electricity network, making it difficult to meet even daily sustenance goals such as lighting homes and cooking or accessing clean water from a pump.[1] Most of this population resided in the rural areas of Asian developing countries, such as India (more than 200 million people) and in sub-Saharan Africa (more than 600 million people).[2] Inadequate lighting severely limited the ability to engage in activities for knowledge enhancement (reading or studying), household management, or income generation. Additionally, buying fuel for lighting often entailed travelling long distances to kerosene vendors, which reduced time available for productive activities and accounted for a significant proportion of total household expenses (about US$1 per week for 3–4 hours of lighting per day), draining away their already limited resources.[3]

The cost of labour and material in laying the essential infrastructure for power grid expansion, estimated to range between US$266 and US$2100 per household, raised the cost of providing energy in these remote areas to a disproportionately high level. Furthermore, the lower-than-average consumption of electricity among low-income households made it economically unattractive for private providers of electricity.[4]

Veriown mapped the access to three essential services at a global level, identifying energy-poor versus energy-rich regions, regions with Internet connectivity versus no connectivity, and regions with access to banking services versus none. The company found that a large overlap existed in terms of the geographical areas for the 1.2 billion who were un-electrified, 3.5 billion that were unconnected, and 2.5 billion who were unbanked. Most of the 'have nots' in all three aspects lived in the developing and impoverished economies of Asia and Africa.

Solar energy: the greener, safer, and cheaper alternative

One lamp of kerosene, which was the accepted mode of generating light among the BoP population, not only released 200 lbs of carbon (CO_2) but also emitted 4,000 lbs of CO_2 worth of black carbon (soot) every year due to incomplete combustion of the fuel. Globally, it amounted to 100–150 million tons of carbon emissions per year.[5] Breathing in air infested with soot particles severely impacted people's health. About 4 million people were found to die every year due to illnesses caused by household air pollution on account of using kerosene and other solid fuels in cooking and for lighting.[6] Kerosene was also a safety hazard, as it could easily trigger fires and cause poisoning.

In contrast, renewable sources of energy, such as solar, wind, or water, were eco-friendly and provided sustainable alternatives to meet the energy needs of both on-grid and off-grid markets (refer to Figure 5.1). Moreover,

Source of Energy	Carbon Dioxide per kWh
Natural gas	0.6 – 2 lbs
Coal	1.5 – 3.6 lbs
Wind	0.02 – 0.04 lbs
Solar	0.07 – 0.2 lbs
Geothermal	0.1 – 0.2 lbs
Hydroelectric	0.1 – 0.5 lbs

Figure 5.1 CO_2 Emissions

Source: RESET, "Renewable Energy—Environmentally Friendly and Low Cost Energy from Inexhaustible Sources", September 2015, https://en.reset.org/knowledge/renewable-energy-environmentally-friendly-and-low-cost-energy-inexhaustible-sources.

the cost of generating solar photovoltaic (PV) electricity had declined considerably over the years, and in 2017, it was at US$0.10 per KwH. Over the next few years, it was expected to become cheaper than the electricity generated by traditional fossil fuels, which was at US$0.05–0.17 per KwH.[7] Additionally, solar PV was a highly modular solution—easier, quicker, and cheaper to install for both on-grid and far off-grid areas, unlike the traditional thermal power that required substantial investment in terms of time, labour, and capital for grid extension.

In India and Africa, regions with good sunlight, use of solar energy was penetrating at a rapid rate. India was estimated to grow its solar capacity by more than ten times, from 13 GW in 2017 to about 150 GW by 2027, and the country was rated as the second most attractive market (after China) for investing in renewable energy.[8] The African market was also showing promising growth, having created a 2 GW solar capacity in 2016 from just 100 MW in 2009.

The bottom of the pyramid opportunity

India had the world's largest BoP market (followed by Nigeria), with annual income levels varying from US$500 to US$3000. In 2015, it was estimated to account for 78 percent of India's population, or 997 million

BOP Income Segment	Population*			Annual Expenditure*		
	Total (millions)	Share (percent of national)	Urban (percent of segment)	Total (US$ million)	Share (percent of national)	Urban (percent of segment)
BOP 3000	31.5	3.2	67.6	89,836.0	6.3	72.4
BOP 2500	68.3	7.0	53.4	159,043.6	11.2	62.4
BOP 2000	147.0	15.1	37.4	264,285.7	18.6	45.4
BOP 1500	309.0	31.8	19.8	394,937.0	27.8	28.2
BOP 1000	349.0	35.9	8.2	288,957.9	20.3	13.8
BOP 500	19.3	2.0	5.6	8,608.2	0.6	8.8

*2005 IFC-WRI Study

Figure 5.2 Veriown Target BoP Segments

people.[9] Veriown planned to initially target the BoP segments that had annual incomes of US$1500 and US$2000 and contributed close to 20 and 30 percent of the annual national expenditure, respectively (refer to Figure 5.2). In the future, it aimed to find ways to reach even further down the BoP.

The three pillars of Veriown's business model

Hyper-innovation

Veriown was conceived with the objective to address the large gap in energy infrastructure, but soon it grew to encompass two other key services—connectivity and microfinance. Internet penetration was considered a key stimulant for any economy. In India, it was estimated that an increase of 10 percent in the rate of growth of Internet users could lead to a 2.4 percent increase in the GDP of the country. However, while Internet penetration in urban India was 65 percent, it was only 20 percent in rural India (70 percent of the country's population lived in rural areas).[10]

Johanns recognised that not only were energy, connectivity, and finance separately essential to help uplift underdeveloped markets economically, they were also related and interdependent. The demand for electricity went beyond the need for lighting. The proliferation of mobile phones brought connectivity to some extent, but people had no reliable means to charge their phones. Inadequate liquidity often limited the ability to use most services, including energy and Internet connections. Thus, in order to create a new rural ecosystem, what was required was a connected solar system model that could make all three services available directly to the homes and small businesses of BoP economies.

The telecom model

The extraordinary growth of mobile phones in developing markets since the early 2000s pointed towards the effectiveness of the business model adopted by the telecom industry. The industry had leapfrogged by introducing mobile devices instead of investing in landlines, a business that would not have been possible without first developing the basic infrastructure, something that most of these markets did not have. Besides, mobile phone penetration was not limited to urban markets. In 2017, according to the Telecom Regulatory Authority of India, there were 499 million mobile subscribers in rural India, of which 109 million owned smartphones. That year, the rural mobile market grew at the rate of 15 percent (year on year) and accounted for 60 percent of the new mobile subscription growth in the country.[11]

Veriown derived two key insights from the telecom model: one, there was a growing demand for electricity at the basic level as mobile owners needed to charge their phones, and two, it would be appropriate to replicate the leapfrog model of the telecom industry in the energy-Internet space and overcome the lack of infrastructure through technical innovation.

Engineering for the invisible woman

The genesis of Veriown's vision was based on a YouTube video of a young woman in Tanzania, working at a health clinic in a tiny village at night, with no access to electricity. According to Johanns, all she had was the light on her phone. She stuck the phone in her mouth to free her hands and used its light to do her work.

This prompted Veriown to engineer a technology-based solution such that a person in a remote part of the world, who had no access to a phone, no access to a grid, no access to the Internet, no access to a bank account, and no access to knowledge could still transact successfully.

Innovation-led strategy

The 'pay as you go' approach

Liquidity-constrained BoP consumers preferred to use kerosene because it allowed them complete flexibility on their usage and payment. They could control their spending by buying only as much kerosene as they had cash (as kerosene could be bought in even small quantities) and control their consumption by turning the kerosene lamps up or down as required. A typical transaction required the customer to carry an empty can and travel some distance to the kerosene seller to buy the fuel.

Veriown replicated this 'pay-as-you-go' mode of transaction in its solution, which had two main components. The first was the ability to convert hard currency into digital currency and credits using a smart card. The smart near-field communication (NFC) card was loaded on the mobile phone using an app, and the customers could use cash to buy credits on the card from a local vendor just like buying kerosene. And second was the use of existing smartphone technology to move the currency and credits into the Veriown system. Moreover, the device, which included a solar panel and battery, could be turned off or changed to low or high as required, allowing the customer to control the amount of credit being used in a manner similar to when using a kerosene lamp. Additionally, it was ensured that the cost of the Veriown transaction remained the same as that of kerosene, while the benefits multiplied.

Veriown's solar home system was a single platform that included the capabilities of smartphone technology, internet-connected solar energy, and cloud-based services. It collaborated with Microsoft to develop the Veriown cloud-based computing platform that integrated all services. Veriown also collaborated with Vodafone, one of the leading telecom providers in rural India, for providing critical last-mile connectivity. The end result was a technologically advanced product, which, besides electricity for lighting and DC-powered devices, allowed customers to charge their phones, access the Internet, view online content, run media, and connect with local fintech services and opportunities.

Micro-lending enabled market

Micro-lending was critical in order to keep the price in reach of the target market. India's biometric identification system—Aadhaar card—had been issued to more than 99 percent of India's total adult population, providing authentic and secured proof of identity for easy processing of consumer loans.[12]

DMI, a leading India-based non-banking financial company (NBFC), with its digital-only and partnership-based model, had 38 partners across fintech start-ups, large digital wallets, and international consumer electronic brands in 2017. Its extensive consumer-lending network processed over 500,000 loans and disbursed over 100,000 loans a month. Partnership with DMI allowed Veriown to offer its solar device to consumers at about the same daily rate as a limited solar power lighting device while also providing access to the Internet, media, and commerce services.

Installation and servicing network

The challenge of entering a market like India was in developing the capability to install, maintain and provide service on a significantly large scale from the very start. The Indian government had authorised installation of certain solar-based lighting devices in rural areas. However, these were allotted under a lottery system, with only 10 percent of the applicants making the cut. The remaining 90 percent of households that made up the unfulfilled consumer demand were a ready target market for Veriown.

In order to service this market, Veriown collaborated with UMG, which had tremendous experience and a good track record in installing solar home lighting systems under government contracts. UMG offered exclusive sales, service, and installation to Veriown through its network of field service personnel and 50 team members at its operations hub in New Delhi. It also enabled toll-free phone customer support to end users through its service centres spread across the states it was active in.

Critical success factors in a BoP market

Sustainable value delivery and product adoption are essential for success in rural markets.

Effectiveness of last-mile distribution

Veriown planned to leverage its partners' networks for selling the product and the credits for NFC-enabled cards and the installation of the device at end-users' home. Furthermore, through DMI enabled micro-lending services, it planned to make its device available to consumers at less than 10 percent (as down payment) of its price. The down payment would be treated as a security deposit for the loan that would pay for the system over a period of five years.

However, intermediaries add to the financial cost of the product being sold. The greater the number of intermediaries, the higher the cost—and this leads to an inflated cost structure. Thus, it was important for Veriown, which had a three-tier distribution channel, to examine its cost structure, determine the incremental cost of three intermediaries, and evaluate if the cost of distribution and financing was high and consider how it could minimise the same. A high cost of intermediaries would lead to either higher pricing for end users or higher expenses for the company if it decided not to pass the costs on to the consumers.

One of the most important criteria was to determine the willingness to pay (WTP) of the consumers. This becomes even more important in BoP markets that have a significantly lower purchasing power, have a lack of reliable income sources, and are dominated by the informal economy. WTP can be defined as the highest price a consumer will pay for one unit of a good or service. For a new product, it is equal to the cost of the best available alternative plus the perceived value of performance differential and thus determines the level of consumer demand for a product at a certain price. An analysis of the WTP is the first step that any business must undertake, as a wrong pricing approach has a direct impact on the adoption of the product and scalability of the business model in BoP markets.

Firms that are purely commercial tend to look at a region's social disadvantage as an opportunity for profit making and hence look at pricing from the perspective of value extraction. A social enterprise, however, aims for a balance between the social mission and the profit motive. Moreover, long-term success in poor markets is possible only when community welfare is kept in mind before the profit motive, or else the adoption of the solution will not be satisfactory in the long run. Most end users in the BoP have to pay higher prices for basic goods and services than those who live in urban areas.

The time and financial cost of accessing these services is much more for them, and they often receive a lower quality of products and service as well. An enterprise like Veriown needs to address these problems by determining the consumers' WTP level and examining how it can reduce the share of the intermediaries without compromising on the product/service quality.

Degree of product adoption

Besides WTP, trust and product characteristics are the key factors that drive product adoption in rural markets.[13]

Trust

Unlike urban markets, consumers in rural areas tend to make most of their decisions based on trust. Low literacy levels and lack of awareness and knowledge make them seek and rely on word of mouth from well-known and trustworthy individuals. In the case of a new product that requires a change in existing buying behaviour and consumption patterns, it is important for the manufacturer to first invest in winning their confidence. Veriown's association with UMG, a well-known and respected brand in the launch markets, and established women-centric village-level entrepreneur networks, were steps in the right direction. However, Veriown should also invest in educating consumers through focused promotional programmes and offer free product trials to overcome any doubts or concerns and demonstrate ease of use.

Product characteristics

The following criteria of an innovation impact the rate of its adoption among users:[14]

- Relative Advantage: The degree to which an innovation is perceived as superior to existing products. Veriown offered a three-in-one solution to the single-use solar lanterns available in the market, enabling users to charge their phones and access the Internet, too. While it offered a clear advantage, it is important to consider that the cost of solar lamps is declining considerably, and there is high penetration of smartphones in Indian rural markets, with mobile data available at dirt-cheap prices. For instance, Reliance Jio, the leading mobile service provider, offers a smartphone with unlimited calls and mobile data for a US$23 deposit (refundable after three years) and less than US$2 per month.[15]

- Compatibility: The degree to which an innovation fits the values and experiences of potential consumers. As rural consumers have been using solar lamps and mobile phones, Veriown's solution is compatible with their lifestyle. However, it would involve a learning process for those who have been using kerosene lamps so far. Also, its NFC card based on credits purchased is something they would have not been exposed to. However, being used to recharging their mobile phone connections, it should be a relatively easy process to understand and adopt.
- Complexity: The degree to which an innovation is difficult to understand or to use. Rural consumers are used to using discrete single services through kerosene vendors and solar lamp manufacturers that work simply on a plug-and-play model. The three-in-one innovation would require them to imbibe a new way of buying and using these services. It is important that the device be simple to use and have highly user-friendly navigation capabilities.
- Divisibility: The degree to which an innovation may be tried on a limited basis. A product trial for a few days is important for consumers to test Veriown's device without having to commit to investing in it.
- Communicability: The degree to which the results of using an innovation can be observed or described to others. Veriown's product allows homes to be lit, phones to be charged, and the Internet accessed and viewed on a screen on top of the device. Thus, the product has high communicability, but it is important for the company to educate consumers about it and demonstrate the benefits through adequate local-level promotions.

Going forward

The BoP segment in developing countries is a strategic and competitive space for Internet-connected energy service providers, with the opportunity to expand both in scale and scope in the future. To begin with, there was huge market demand for a product that used solar battery storage to make electricity available at a fraction of the cost. Moreover, it enabled rural consumers to have reliable and cheap access to the Internet, thereby opening up this large consumer segment that was hitherto inaccessible to online service providers. Thus, even before the launch, Veriown was eagerly sought out as a key partner by a number of companies, including a digital media company that provided entertainment content and a digital radio network that offered radio services for rural homes.

Once operational in India, Veriown planned to replicate its model in Africa and other rural areas of the world, including those in the developed markets. However, the future growth and direction of the company rested on its ability to deliver effectively in the launch markets in India.

Notes

1 Lily Odarno, *1.2 Billion People Lack Electricity. Increasing Supply Alone Won't Fix the Problem*, World Resources Institute, March 2017, www.wri.org/blog/2017/03/12-billion-people-lack-electricity-increasing-supply-alone-wont-fix-problem.

2 Rebekah Shirley, "Millions of Urban Africans Still Don't Have Electricity: Here's What Can Be Done", *The Conversation*, April 2018, http://theconversation.com/millions-of-urban-africans-still-dont-have-electricity-heres-what-can-be-done-92211; Rajesh Kumar Singh and Saket Sundria, "Living in the Dark: 240 Million Indians Have No Electricity", *Bloomberg*, January 2017, www.bloomberg.com/news/features/2017-01-24/living-in-the-dark-240-million-indians-have-no-electricity.

3 Rainbow Power Company, "Fuel Based Lighting", www.rpc.com.au/information/developing-countries/fuel-based-lighting.html.

4 Marian Willuhn, "BNEF: Micro-Grids Could 'Leapfrog' the Grids for Universal Power Supply", *PV Magazine*, July 2018, www.pv-magazine.com/2018/07/16/bnef-micro-grids-could-leapfrog-the-grids-for-universal-power-supply/.

5 John Barrie, "Negative Impacts of Kerosene Lamps", *LinkedIn*, January 2018, www.linkedin.com/pulse/negative-impacts-kerosene-lamps-john-barrie.

6 World Health Organisation, "Household Air Pollution and Health", May 2018, www.who.int/news-room/fact-sheets/detail/household-air-pollution-and-health.

7 Dominic Dudley, "Renewable Energy Will Be Consistently Cheaper Than Fossil Fuels by 2020, Report Claims", *Forbes*, January 2018, www.forbes.com/sites/dominicdudley/2018/01/13/renewable-energy-cost-effective-fossil-fuels-2020/#1bf468084ff2.

8 Ian Clover, "India to Reach 57 Percent Renewable Penetration by 2027, Forecasts Government", *PV Magazine*, December 2016, www.pv-magazine.com/2016/12/21/india-to-reach-57-renewable-penetration-by-2027-forecasts-government/; Manu Balachandran, "It's Smarter to Invest in Renewable Energy in India Than the US", *Quartz India*, May 2017, https://qz.com/india/984486/its-smarter-to-invest-in-renewable-energy-in-india-than-the-us/.

9 The Economic Times, "Bottom of the Pyramid Market Stands at $1.2 Trillion", 17 April 2007, https://economictimes.indiatimes.com/news/economy/indicators/bottom-of-the-pyramid-market-stands-at-1–2-trillion/articleshow/1962467.cms; Unitus Ventures, "Defining 'Base of the Economic Pyramid' in India", https://unitus.vc/resources/defining-base-of-the-economic-pyramid-in-india/.

10 Vishal Krishna, "Internet Penetration May Be Rising, but the Urban-Rural Digital Divide Remains a Reality in India", *Your Story*, March 2018, https://yourstory.com/2018/03/internet-penetration-may-rising-urban-rural-digital-divide-remains-reality-india/; Amit Kapoor, "Tapping the Telecom Sector for Next Phase of GDP Growth: View", *ET Telecom*, December 2017, https://telecom.economictimes.indiatimes.com/news/tapping-the-telecom-sector-for-next-phase-of-gdp-growth-view/62131080.

11 Meghna Sharma, "Mobile Handset Penetration: Why Rural Consumer Is Not Rural Anymore", *Financial Express*, August 2017, www.financialexpress.com/industry/mobile-handset-penetration-why-rural-consumer-is-not-rural-anymore/788513/.

12 Mahendra Singh, "99 Percent of Indians over 18 Now Have Aadhaar Cards", *The Times of India*, January 2017, http://timesofindia.indiatimes.com/articleshow/56820818.cms?utm_source=contentofinterest&utm_medium=text&utm_campaign=cppst "https://timesofindia.indiatimes.com/india/99-of-indians-over-18-now-have-aadhaar/articleshow/56820818.cms.

13 Philip Kotler and Gary Armstrong, *Principles of Marketing: A Global Perspective*, Harlow: Pearson, 2012.

14 Ibid.

15 First Post, "Jio Phone, Free with RS 1,500 Deposit, Unlimited 4G Data Launched: All You Need to Know about Mukesh Ambani's Smartphone", 21 July 2017, www.firstpost.com/india/watch-jio-phone-free-with-rs-1500-deposit-unlimited-4g-data-launched-all-you-need-to-know-about-mukesh-ambanis-smartphone-3839871.html.

6

GREAT WOMEN: INTEGRATING MICRO-ENTREPRENEURS INTO THE REGIONAL VALUE CHAIN

Howard Thomas and Lakshmi Appasamy

The case, set in mid-2017, traces the evolution of a gender-responsive regional multi-stakeholder platform called GREAT Women ASEAN, dedicated to the economic empowerment of women micro-producers. In 2009, Jeannie Javelosa and her friends, Regina Francisco and Pacita Juan, founded ECHOsi, a non-profit foundation that helped micro-producers improve their products and market base through market-linking and business support services. The Philippines Commission on Women (PCW) partnered with ECHOsi to implement the GREAT Women Programme (GWP), a Women Economic Empowerment (WEE) programme funded by the Canadian government. As the GWP garnered commercial traction, its ownership was transferred to ECHOsi.

The United States Agency for International Development (USAID) eventually identified the GWP as an ideal WEE model to be replicated in ASEAN. It enlisted ECHOsi to help integrate women micro-entrepreneurs (WMEs) into the regional value chain. As the impact model scaled, Javelosa had to prepare for the risks involved in franchising the social enterprise and also find the means of funding the expansion.

This case highlights the challenges faced by micro-entrepreneurs, particularly WMEs in ASEAN. It discusses the key characteristics and objectives of social enterprise along the social and

DOI: 10.4324/9781003203582-7

commercial continuum, the funding options available, and the management of risks pertaining to social franchising.

It was June 2017, and Jeannie E. Javelosa (Jeannie), the principal representative of the 'GREAT Women' brand, an offshoot of the Gender Responsive Economic Actions for the Transformation of Women Project—GREAT Women (GW) Project, was on a flight to Manila. She was returning after a weeklong trip across Southeast Asia to evaluate potential partners who would be confederated into the programme's regional spinoff. The GW Project, which was sponsored by the Canadian government, along with other private partners, had helped women-led Filipino microenterprises gain access to commercial markets. Following successful outcomes in the Philippines, the United States Agency for International Development (USAID) had identified GW as an ideal Women Economic Empowerment (WEE) model to be replicated regionally. Hence, since 2015, the programme had started to evolve into a regional initiative called GREAT Women ASEAN Initiative (GWAI) to leverage the market opportunities in the emergent ASEAN Economic Community (AEC).

While Jeannie was proud that what had started as a modest entrepreneurial endeavour had morphed to a regional development initiative, she was concerned about the challenges involved in expanding it into a regional multi-stakeholder platform. She was assessing her potential moves in response to the challenges in institutionalising the model regionally, and she knew that balancing profitability with the social mission of the project would not be an easy feat.

A private enterprise's tryst with social mission

Courting the cause

In 2008, Jeannie and her friends Regina Francisco (Reena) and Pacita Juan (Chit)—also known as the ECHOtrio—had launched ECHOstore under a private limited company called Earth Life Store Supply Inc. As a pioneer concept store selling health and personal care products and speciality food items, ECHOstore promoted the cause of sustainability, fair trade, and responsible sourcing. Each cofounder had unique expertise garnered from her work experience and the diverse independent community development projects that she had been engaged in. Their combined experience, knowledge, and network of professionals, donors, governmental, and non-governmental agencies created a synergistic intangible capital for the venture. When they launched ECHOstore, the idea was to tap into this intangible capital and bridge the gap between the Filipino microenterprises and the market.

Located in a high-footfall mall in Manila, ECHOstore successfully tapped into the discerning, environmentally conscious customers and provided the much-needed branding, positioning, advertising, and marketing boost to the otherwise plain yet superior-quality exotic produces of Filipino microenterprises. The ECHOtrio also augmented the market base by running multimedia campaigns that spread knowledge and awareness among the public on a sustainable, healthy, and green lifestyle.

Eventually, the venture expanded to ECHOgroup that included ECHOmarket, which sold fresh organic produce, and ECHOcafe, which served organic food and beverages. The manifesto 'self, society and the planet' guided the group; it catered to the 'self' by dealing in healthy, natural and whole foods; supported 'society' through innovative and inclusive collaborations; and helped the 'planet' by promoting sustainable and natural products.

Over time, ECHOstore transformed into a logistical interface between bulk buyers and the microenterprises. Most microenterprises were typically unorganised and therefore lacked the requisite registration and licenses to issue invoices to buyers. For example, a leading commercial departmental store in the Philippines selling Filipino heritage products engaged ECHOstore to supply products produced by local communities. The communities benefited from regular orders from the departmental store, while ECHOstore, as an intermediary, provided documentation and invoicing service. Also, most microenterprises lacked adequate labelling and packaging of their products and could not retail via regular channels. ECHOstore's house brand came to the rescue of such micro-entrepreneurs whose volumes were inconsistent, small, or lacked the resources to package their produce. Aided by ECHOstore's interface, the micro-entrepreneurs enjoyed a steady flow of orders, shorter cash-conversion-cycles, and improved marketability. ECHOstore thus successfully straddled its social and business mission, and the media dubbed it the epitome of a social enterprise (SE).

Soon, the ECHOtrio realised that women dominated the venture's entire value chain, and it made sense to play the gender card and focus only on women micro-entrepreneurs (WMEs) for the desired social impact.

Bonded with the cause

Over time, ECHOstore had to turn down requests to carry products from several WMEs and NGOs due to lack of visual appeal or design finesse. This made them recognise the gap between the offerings of the micro-entrepreneurs and the market requirements. Determined to fill the gap, the ECHOtrio started volunteering their time and expertise to train the WMEs to adapt their product designs to market requirements, reaching out to WMEs whose products were outside the product mix of ECHOstore. They were soon approached by NGOs and other organisations working with micro-entrepreneurs and marginalised communities to improve the viability of their developmental works. Corporations and educational institutions also invited the ECHOtrio to talk and conduct workshops on sustainable lifestyles and ECHOgroup's social mission.

In 2009, with help from angel investors, the ECHOtrio set up a non-profit entity, ECHOsi Foundation (ECHOsi), with an investment of PHP 1 million (US$21,523).[1] ECHOsi's agenda was to create a loop of sustainability whereby micro-entrepreneurs, government agency representatives, designers and merchandise developers, retailers, and conscious consumers were integrated into the value chain by focusing on what really mattered to each stakeholder, independently and collectively.

The ECHOsi Foundation had two core programmes:

ECHOdesign Lab

The ECHOdesign Lab (EDL) conducted workshops in which WMEs were taught about market-driven product development. The training programmes had three segments—design clinics that helped the communities with design or material directions, working drawings, and ideas for development; critique sessions that provided insights on product intervention, packaging improvement, and variant development; and business development sessions that focused on licensing, branding, certifications, and labelling.

ECHOteach

This programme engaged the stakeholders through workshops, forums, and talks to teach them the importance and fundamentals of a sustainable lifestyle. A wide range of mass media and social media channels were used to disseminate information and knowledge on green philosophy and the need for supporting WMEs. The buzz created by the initiatives of ECHOteach improved sales at the ECHOstore.

The ECHOstore thus functioned as a for-profit trading entity, while ECHOsi was a non-profit focusing on developmental works. The ECHOstore formed the basis of the developmental works of ECHOsi and generated economic benefits for the community, while ECHOsi fortified the brand equity of the ECHOstore.

Public–private nexus

The empowerment of women had been at the top of the national agenda in the Philippines for a very long time, evidenced by the establishment of the Philippine Commission on Women (PCW) in 1975.[2] The promulgation of the Magna Carta of Women in 2010 went a long way to eliminate discrimination against women by recognising, protecting, fulfilling, and promoting the rights of Filipino women, especially those in the marginalised sectors.

The bulk of the economy, over 95 percent, was represented by the private sector, of which micro, small, and medium enterprises (MSMEs) accounted for over 91 percent.[3] More than half of these MSMEs were owned by women, and they accounted for a major part of the existing employment and new jobs in the private sector. Hence, the development of MSMEs was identified as the key driver of economic competitiveness and gender equality that would curb the constraints that impeded the economic participation of women.

The PCW was in charge of institutionalising gender-mainstreaming efforts for the MSMEs. As a part of these efforts, the PCW was running Phase I of the Canadian-sponsored WEE GW project that was launched in 2007, which focused on working with local government units to create and reform policies with gender sensitivity to create an enabling environment for women's livelihood and economic empowerment. The PCW was looking for private partners to support its pursuit in creating an enabling enterprise ecosystem for women and thus approached ECHOsi. PCW sought the partnership of ECHOsi Foundation to provide commercial input and product innovation support.

Embedding into the value chain

The following challenges precluded the WMEs from the value chain:

- Inadequate knowledge of market requirements
- Lack of opportunities to upgrade skills
- Lack of capacity and resources
- Risk aversion and subsistence mindset
- Poor organisation and lack of supportive policy framework
- Shallow networks

The GW initiative educated the beneficiaries on market fundamentals (different markets, trends, distribution channels, evolving consumer behaviour, and the market potential for speciality products) and business fundamentals (such as creating fabric swatches and samples of products for securing orders, banking and financing basics).

Most WMEs lacked the motivation to grow their business. They were unwilling to organise formally, develop professionalism, improve capacities, or standardise quality. Such drawbacks precluded them from being embedded into the value chain. Inspiring success stories, mentoring programmes, interactive events, and tradeshows organised by the GW project boosted the beneficiaries' confidence and pride in their products and fostered a desire to organise and grow their business. Most WMEs lived in rural areas and were largely dominated by men, lacked exposure, and were burdened with domestic responsibilities. Creating a network of sisterhood on a 'women-helping-women' model facilitated the WMEs to approach and interact with one another and ask for help without the sociocultural barriers.

The feedback and interventions at GW workshops helped the beneficiaries improve the marketability of their products by attuning the features of their products to the market trends and needs. Sociocultural limitations constrained WMEs' mobility and had precluded them from developing business networks essential for growth. The GW workshops paved the way to networking and association and helped them to share business and enterprise information.

ECHOsi also unified the various government agencies and local government units, whose developmental works were siloed, under the GW project, resulting in a national platform. This enabled developmental programs to be approached and implemented seamlessly with a gender lens. WMEs, mostly being unorganised, lacked the power to drive transformative conversations and dialogues. The GW platform provided much-needed advocacy, urging policymakers to conduct a gender audit of existing policies to identify gender-based constraints.

ECHOtrio brought commercial partners into the ecosystem. They offered practical training, shared intelligence on current market trends and commercial demands on design, and eventually brought the WMEs into their value chain as suppliers and thus propelled them into high-growth sectors.

Charting a clear course

The GW project successfully embedded WMEs into the value chain by addressing the gaps in their mindset, skills, and product design, as well as the inadequacies in the enterprise support framework and ecosystem. The GW brand was launched in 2013 to celebrate the culmination of the Phase 1 of the project. The GW brand helped in integrating the products of the beneficiaries under one collective identity. Products that sold under the GW brand name earned a premium price. Soon after, as commercial and profit-making activities were not within their ambit, the PCW and its Canadian donor agency handed over the ownership of the brand and its mark to ECHOsi, which later entrusted the brand's commercialisation to Earth Life Store Supply Inc (ELSS). The ownership transfer provided greater autonomy to ECHOtrio to manage the brand.

Phase 1 of the C$6 million (US$5.17 million) GW project had supported 7,331 beneficiaries. ECHOsi had provided business and product training to 3,655 beneficiaries, improved 90 products, and provided access to high-end retail markets for 11 products. It continued to be funded by donations from private entities, and ECHOstore contributed 10 percent of its net profits to ECHOsi.

Going regional

The impressive results achieved in Phase I of the GW programme led the Canadian government to launch Phase II with an intensified role for private-sector players, led by ECHOsi. Later in 2013, when the GW model was presented as a best practice for WEE at the high-level policy dialogue of the

Policy Partnership for Women and the Economy (PPWE), the USAID picked the GW model to be replicated among ASEAN member countries. Again, ECHOsi was selected as the lead private-sector partner.

Social impact projects, during their scale-up, must be wary of the non-financial impediments that could potentially lead to impact dilution or even failure (Hartman and Linn identify political, policy, organisational, cultural, partnership, and learning as non-challenges that impede scaling).[4]

Securing buy-in

Jeannie presented the idea of a regional platform at the 2014 meeting of the US-ASEAN Business Alliance for Competitive SMEs (Business Alliance), where women business owners and leaders unreservedly endorsed the platform's agenda. Soon after, the GWAI was presented at the 2015 ASEAN-SME Summit in Malaysia and cemented the allegiance of the women entrepreneurs and business leaders to the GW Platform, which was essentially built on the 'women-helping-women' model. The GWAI also attracted the attention of other private-sector donors such as UPS and Facebook and government agencies from countries such as Australia and Japan.

While expanding within the Philippines, private foundations and donor agencies had provided the critical philanthropic capital to the GW Platform, and their endorsements opened doors to networks and resources. As the platform expanded regionally, the backing of the foundations and donor agencies brought added synergies. GW could tap into the convening power of foundations and donor agencies to secure commitment and support from government officials, partnerships, and alliances from practitioners in the ecosystem and create awareness of the mission and the model. GW could also accommodate different risk profiles by blending grants, donations and equity investments. When expanding into new markets where SEs had poor reliability records, the validation rendered by foundations and donor agencies improved GW's funding and partnership prospects.

Creating a collective

The GW Platform aimed to build loops of sustainability by securing committed partnerships from diverse stakeholders along the value chain, including local government units, retailers, and media, as well as enterprise and retail consumers. It also included impact investors and angel investors to facilitate access to capital for the women entrepreneurs.

In early 2017, ECHOsi started building a GW Collective of women entrepreneurs to develop products collaboratively and market them under the GW brand. To qualify as a member of GW Collective and part of the GW platform, prospects—whether they were designers, artists, communities, or entrepreneurs—were expected to subscribe to and imbibe the philosophy of fair-trade and inclusive business and workforce policies. They also had to be majority owned by women, or a majority of their workforce had to be women. The members would source from supply chains comprising WMEs or community livelihood projects producing exclusive collections. The development programmes of the GW platform would assist the communities and WMEs in the members' value chain.

Expanding footprint

By mid-2017, the GW Platform had expanded its network to Malaysia, Indonesia, Myanmar, Laos PDR, and Cambodia. ELSS licensed the GW brand to GREAT Women Philippines Corporation, an independent trading unit set up for the Philippines market. The licensee model would be replicated in the ASEAN market, and soon the licensees would share a portion of their profits with ECHOsi.

The moot point—corporate social responsibility or social enterprise

Kim Alter has proposed the sustainability spectrum to assess an organisation based on the degree of orientation in terms of motive, accountability, and use of income.[5]

ECHOsi as a corporation's social responsibility practice

Although ECHOstore was sharing 10 percent of its profits with ECHOsi, based on its privately held nature and potential to distribute surplus, ECHOstore could be placed on the extreme right of the sustainability spectrum as a purely commercial for-profit entity. Its contribution to the ECHOsi could be deemed a unique selling proposition to appeal its environmentally conscious customer base.

Though an off-shoot of ECHOstore to augment its supply side, ECHOsi should not be viewed as a mere extension of the supply-side enhancement measure. As it extended mentoring to beneficiaries who produced items outside the product-mix of ECHOstore, its commitment to the social mission should not be understated. ECHOsi, as a non-trading, advocacy-driven entity, financed by funds and donations from private entities and donor agencies, could be deemed a corporate social responsibility (CSR) practice of ECHOstore in the sustainability spectrum. Arguably, they were 'doing good to do well.'

GW as a platform was a development initiative spearheaded by government agencies and sponsoring foreign government agencies in which ECHOsi rendered its service as a private-sector partner in implementing projects. When the model is replicated, the platform will remain an initiative, while ECHOsi receiving donations from licensees would be on the extreme left as a non-profit entity. However, it could eventually even become a non-profit with income-generating activities if it gets dividend payouts from licensees as their shareholder.

ECHOsi as a non-profit arm of the SE ECHOstore

If more liberal definitions of SEs that support profit maximisation and dividend payouts are considered, then ECHOstore could be regarded as a SE providing market-linking services for the beneficiaries of the ECHOsi. Thus, ECHOstore would be in the middle of the sustainability spectrum generating blended benefits. Besides contributing 10 percent of its profits, it was also sharing the tangible and intangible resources with ECHOsi. Essentially, they were 'doing well to do good.' By bridging the gap and building an ecosystem with the mentoring and curatorial programmes, ECHOsi manifests the traits of a non-profit.

Alter identifies three ways of integrating a SE with a non-profit organisation:

- *Internal:* Commercial activities of the SE overlap with and finance the non-profit's programmes. Resources and management are shared based on agreement.

- *Embedded:* Commercial activities of the SE are the same as the programmes of the non-profit and service the beneficiaries of the non-profits.
- *External:* Commercial activities of the SE and the non-profit's programmes are separate and may or may not be related to the non-profit's mission. The SE funds the programmes of the non-profit, and the entities are legally distinct.

Based on legal structure, shared mission, and resource sharing between the two, it can be established that ECHOsi is a non-profit arm of the ECHOstore, a SE. Each of the GW licensees in the emergent regional GW platform would be a separate SE, with the platform itself remaining a developmental initiative to create an enabling regional ecosystem for the WMEs.

Funding: key considerations

Clear value proposition: The funders, excluding those making grants, gifts, and donations, often have both altruistic and financial interests. Therefore, the social value proposition and measurable impact metrics must be clearly articulated.

Mission alignment: The funders, recipient, and management must be clearly aligned with the mission. Mission drift could disenchant workers or investors who were primarily drawn by the social mission.

Disclosures: By having proper disclosures on revenue generation, profit generation, distribution, and reinvestment; clear accounting policies; and appropriate financial structuring, organisations can prevent donor attrition.

Tax consideration: If income-generating activities exceed a certain threshold, the organisation may be exposed to taxation and result in a curb in the tax privileges of donors.

Structure: Organisations structured as charities or companies limited by guarantee cannot raise equity capital.

Costs: The cost of raising funds or loans may outweigh the benefits, and it would adversely affect the scope of impact or the quality of the impact created.

GW's evolving platform has two arms—an enterprise arm engaged in trading and a platform delivering the social mission through developmental works. With a proven revenue model, the commercial arm has a wider option of conventional business finance, such as equity, debt, and convertible debt, as well as the ability to tap into other emerging options depending on their availability in the market where it operates. It would be challenging for the platform to fund; though it presently has the backing of international government and corporation donor agencies, it may not be supported perpetually and must be prepared for the withdrawal of aid agencies.

In its early stage, it is difficult to quantify impacts or determine metrics. Bringing impact investors or other newer forms of funding options on board would be challenging without any track record in the new geographies. Alternatively, securing strong local partnerships with mission-aligned partners could build credibility, and with strong donor backing, the financing cost could be partially offset. However, it must deal with investor intrusion. As a new entrant in unknown geographies, the critical question is: What does it value? The freedom to pursue programmes critical to social issues that have discernible impact, or to achieve the milestones and metrics stated by its investors?

The GREAT challenge

As the GW social impact model scales and evolves into a regional multi-stakeholder platform, its spirit, mission, and perception must be preserved. Measures must be put in place to manage the challenges involved in building a regional multi-stakeholder platform, financing the expansion, and, more importantly, managing the odds of scaling up an enterprise with a social mission.

Notes

1 US$1 = PHP 46.46 as of January 2009.

2 Brigitte Spaeth, Jean Franco, and Sam Raras, "Enhancing Competitiveness through Gender Mainstreaming: The Role and Status of Women and Men in MSME Development in the Philippines", PSP SMEDSEP, GTZ, German Federal Ministry for Economic Cooperation and Development, August 2010.

3 Ibid.

4 Arntraud Hartmann and Johannes F. Linn, *Scaling Up: A Framework for Development Effectiveness from Literature and Practice*, Wolfensohn Center for Development, The Brookings Institution, 31 October 2008, https://papers.ssrn.com/sol3/papers.cfm?abstract_id=1301625.

5 Kim Alter, *Social Enterprise Typology*, Virtue Ventures, www.4lenses.org/setypology/hybrid_spectrum.

7

HOMAGE: HARNESSING TECHNOLOGY TO TACKLE SINGAPORE'S AGEING CHALLENGES

Jonathan Chang and Lakshmi Appasamy

Set in 2018, this case follows Gillian Tee and Lily Phang, the co-founders of Homage, a Singapore-based start-up providing on-demand home care service to the elderly. The government was promoting families as the first line of care for the elderly. However, tending to elderly family members was affecting family caregivers. Such informal caregiving was also causing discomfort to the elderly care recipients. Incumbent care agencies relied on foreign workers due to the shortage of a trained local workforce, their conventional operating model was less effective in helping the care recipients, and the coordination between care recipients and care professionals was erratic and tedious.

Homage's smartphone-based application addressed these problems by matching elderly care recipients and care professionals. It provided a seamless and cost-effective care service while creating flexible income opportunities for those who had left the workforce. After gaining ground in the market and securing funds for growth, Tee and Phang were preparing to scale Homage.

This case guides readers on social impact analysis of demographic change, adopting technology for social innovation, applying social innovation for systemic change, building social enterprises for social innovation, using grants and private capital for social innovation, and choosing the right scaling strategy.

Two weeks had passed since the start of the 2018 Chinese New Year (CNY)—the year of the Dog had dawned. At half-past eight in the evening,

DOI: 10.4324/9781003203582-8

Gillian Tee (Tee) and Lily Phang (Phang) sat together in Homage's office, which was nestled on the third floor of a quaint little shophouse in Chinatown, Singapore. Launched in 2016, Homage was a tech start-up that provided on-demand home care services to seniors in Singapore. Tee was its CEO, and Phang was the COO.

The Homage app linked seniors in need of home care services to a pool of inactive but trained nurses and certified caregivers who preferred flexible working hours. Seniors were able to access home care services on demand at affordable prices, while the caregivers enjoyed flexible work hours and incomes. By leveraging technology, Homage was able to activate dormant resources and provide a solution to the far-reaching impacts of a rapidly ageing population (refer to Figure 7.1).

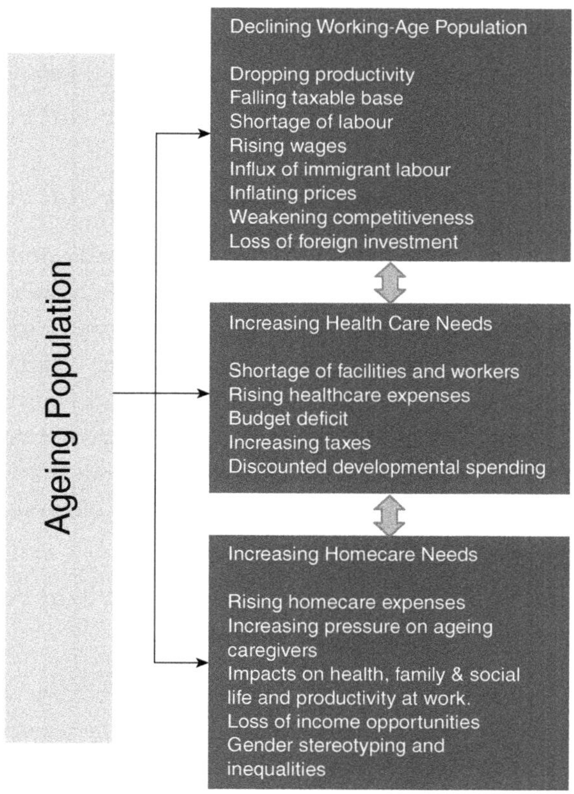

Figure 7.1 The Socio-Economic Impact of Ageing Population

Tee and Phang were reviewing the service fulfilment reports for the CNY period, during which the demand for home care service had spiked, but Homage's supply of freelance caregivers had become tight, as some of the caregivers were out of town or busy with the festivities. Tee and Phang heaved a sigh of relief as they realised that despite the supply constraints during the festive period, the fulfilment of service requests was seamless. While Homage had nearly perfected the product and the backend infrastructure, it now had to gear up for growth.

Growing demand for home care

Singapore was preparing for an ageing crisis. The immediate concern of the government was to contain the healthcare costs and the stress on healthcare infrastructure and personnel by focusing on families and communities as the first line of care rather than hospitals and eldercare homes. The government had several schemes to help families care for their elders in the home environment.

Challenges of informal care

Largely speaking, family members provided home-based care for seniors, as full-time caregivers were expensive. Though this was cheaper than institutional care, the demands of caregiving affected the productivity and physical and mental wellbeing of the caregivers.[1] The caregivers, mostly women, had to stay out of the workforce. As most informal caregivers were not trained in geriatric caregiving, the care recipients also experienced discomfort. Some families resorted to respite services offered by nursing homes and eldercare centres or ended up employing foreign domestic workers (FDWs) who lacked adequate training and experience.

The gaps in service

The demand for professional home care service providers was growing. However, due to the tight domestic labour market, the agencies providing such services had to rely on immigrant healthcare workers.[2] Despite the apparent labour crunch, Singapore had significant untapped resources—more than 5,000 registered nurses were not practising due to family commitments.[3] Government efforts to make non-practising nurses return to the workforce led to moderate results because the long working hours and the lack of flexibility of fulltime jobs acted as major deterrents.[4]

Meanwhile, there was another pool of latent and untrained workers who preferred flexible work arrangements. Deploying this pool after some training could potentially serve those seniors who just needed trained caregivers to help with activities of daily living such as bathing, eating, mobility, and other social activities. Traditional agency models that manually matched such caregivers to care recipients resulted in poor matching, gaps in communication, and service latency, leading to frustration among caregivers and recipients.

A personal calling

The co-founders of Homage had their own unique and personal experiences that compelled them to find a solution for this social issue. After spending 15 years in the United States, Tee had returned to Singapore to be with her ageing mother. Her personal experience of looking after her mother made her realise that the country's demographic profile was changing quickly and would eventually require a transformation in the caregiving industry. While in the United States, she had co-founded Rocketrip, a platform that helped client companies reduce their travel expenses by incentivising employees who beat the budget generated by Rocketrip's predictive algorithm. She wanted to replicate Rocketrip's model of extracting value out of dormant resources using algorithms to analyse and match layers of data for home care services.

Phang had over 20 years of experience working as a healthcare executive in several countries globally. While working at the Singapore General Hospital, she had observed that several elderly patients were hospitalised for non-serious conditions, thus causing stress on the healthcare resources and infrastructure. The fatigue and stress that she experienced while caring for the elders in her family and her observations at work prompted her to explore means of providing efficient home care services.

Meanwhile, Tong Duong, then an undergraduate at Singapore Management University's (SMU) School of Information Systems, was also keen on tapping into technology to create a trusted marketplace for care professionals and seniors. He faced challenges while taking care of his diabetic grandmother.

Based on his personal experience and knowledge gained from volunteering at the voluntary welfare organisations (VWOs) that serviced the destitute seniors in the community, he had developed a proposal for an online marketplace that matched the elderly to potential caregivers. The proposal won several cash awards from foundations and organisations that promoted innovations that address social issues.

Tee, Phang, and Duong were working independently on their respective ideas and were scouting for potential partners and investors in the start-up and venture capital community. There, their common mentor introduced them to each other. Discovering their shared vision and potential synergies, the trio teamed up.

Homage home care on demand

The founders partnered with VWOs and offered free caregiving services to gain a deeper understanding of the supply and demand side of the market. The volunteering helped them realise that most of the homecare needs were not clinical and many of the seniors needed psychosocial support, much of which could be fulfilled by activating the latent resources of housewives, retirees, and students. However, technology was critical to integrate and efficiently deploy the diverse and dispersed workforce. Their efforts led to an innovative and intuitive matching algorithm that fundamentally altered how home care services are accessed and delivered. By connecting the dormant workforce that needed flexible income-earning opportunities and the elderly population that needed home care services, a social capital capable of fulfilling the mutual needs was created.

The application

The app mimicked the asset-light models of taxi booking apps. Harnessing smart technology, web engineering, and mobile computing to match care recipients and caregivers, Homage offered a suite of services ranging from nursing care and daily living to therapy. The user-friendly app ensured accurate, quick, seamless, and stress-free booking, acceptance, delivery, and reporting of home care services. The care recipients were referred to as Care Owners (the seniors themselves) or Care Managers (family members of the seniors), and caregivers were referred to as Care Pros.

The Care Owners/Managers and the Care Pros used separate apps to book, accept, and manage appointments. The Care Owners/Care Managers could request *ad hoc* sessions or schedule regular sessions. Based on their preferences, types of service required, medical history, and current medical condition, the powerful matching algorithm quickly scanned across more than 50 variables such as language, gender, location, and experience to find the best Care Pro match to be assigned to the Care Owner. The Care Pro applicants were carefully screened and had to undergo a rigorous selection process. Upon selection, the Care Pros went through training and onboarding sessions conducted by Homage's clinical care operations.

Technology as an enabler of social innovation

Innovation need not necessarily be an invention; it could just be an optimisation of design or delivery mechanisms or a replacement of an outdated process to produce fundamentally better products or services to the beneficiaries.[5] Given this definition of innovation, we can evaluate the role of technology. In most innovations, standard technology acts as a supporting element, but some innovations would not be possible without technology, and in such cases, the technology involved is specialised, as in the case of Homage.

In the innovation value chain, technology and people synergise the innovation process and technology acts as an enabler from the ideation stage to product launch because of its unique capabilities. People essentially play a more significant role in the delivery of the innovation due to the unique human capabilities that cannot be imitated/simulated by technology.[6]

In Homage's case, technology is the critical enabler to collect, integrate, synthesise, and systematise data relating to both Care Owners and Care Pros. Technology is used to match and allocate Care Pros to Care Owners. Manually matching and allocating Care Pros to Care Owners would be tedious and resource intensive, but technology can improve the operational efficiency and significantly reduce the resource inputs and cost. Data management is critical for an efficient and seamless workflow; if done manually, the data would most likely remain fragmented and disparate across the databases. Technology-enabled real-time management of data and communication among the participants along the value chain helps in making informed operational decisions. When compared to a conventional model, the technology used in Homage reduces the workload on the staff and improves the working conditions of the Care Pros by giving them the ability to choose service requests that best fit their priorities and requirements.

Competitive advantage

Inimitable supply capability

A couple of similar apps were launched around the same time as Homage. Unlike Homage, which differentiated its offerings by specifically targeting the geriatric market, the other apps catered to all market segments. In addition, Homage had built a robust pool of carefully selected, well-trained care professionals and had set high standards for its service. Unlike the care providers of its competitors, Homage's Care Pros were locals who spoke the languages and dialects of the Care Owners; this made the seniors very comfortable and families feel at ease.

Technology

Homage had 500 Care Pros, and each worked around 20 hours a week visiting different Care Owners. Using data analytics, the vast amount of data on Care Owners and Care Pros was turned into actionable information, and the platform's intelligent algorithm ensured seamless operations. The automation process ensured utmost precision in matching, assigning, and, when needed, reassigning of service requests, therefore optimising the work and incomes of Care Pros. Such automation helped to control operating expenses and maintain service efficiency and quality. The technology also contributed to customer retention on both sides of the chain.

Core competency

Given the resource constraints, the co-founders had built a team with comprehensive skills. Hence, half of Homage's technical team, led by Tee, comprised engineers who were trained in artificial intelligence (AI), machine learning, and neuro-linguistic programming. The dynamic capability of the team maximised the productivity of Homage's internal resources. Its access to external networks and expertise facilitated exclusive services at below-market price.

Vaulting the roadblock

Angels to rescue

Homage had been endowed with several grants from the government and private foundations. Such grants helped it develop the app, but by September 2016, soon after launching the app, it was running low on its reserves. Improvisations to the app were ongoing, and given the workload on the small team, there was no time to prepare their pitch to venture capitalists. Determined to stay away from milestone-intensive venture funding that would likely frustrate the already stretched team or detract the company from a dynamic growth path, they looked for angel investors.

The contacts Tee had developed in the investors' circle while in the US introduced her to a robust network of investors in Singapore, and they came to the rescue of Homage. The angel funds empowered them to shift gears and gain momentum for the fundraising exercise. Homage successfully secured US$1.2 million in March 2017, and it quickly expanded its technical team and its service offerings to include therapy sessions.

Role of private capital and grants in driving innovation[7]

Mainstream venture capital and private equity investors have become receptive towards social innovations that are capable of triggering systemic change. Though nascent, private equity has the potential to shift and distribute the responsibility of social welfare from the government and the third sector to the private sector. Some innovations are overlooked because of the high cost or the low risk-tolerance level of the government and organisations in the third sector. Private equity can absolve this risk aversion and foster innovation but in the process could likely undermine the contributions of the third sector in building a strong civil society.

Grants and private capital of social investors play a vital role in promoting social innovations. However, they come into play at different stages of the innovation lifecycle.

- Private grants foster innovation by enhancing risk tolerance of the innovators at the iterative stage. Public finance is too stringent or lacks sectoral knowledge and understanding of market systems. Private investors, keen on returns, invariably support later-stage innovations. Thus, the much-needed 'patient capital' comes from grants.

- Private grants fund multiple innovators that compete with each other and bring market forces to bear on social innovations to moot social change.
- While public grants and private investors are keen on funding only non-localised scalable innovations, private grants are flexible and can work with large and small innovators as well as innovations that are highly localised in frontier markets.
- Private grants that are typically endowed by large philanthropic foundations and corporations are capable of furthering cross-sector fertilisation and exchange of ideas and resources. Hence, they accelerate the innovation process and the diffusion mechanism.
- In the growth and diffusion stage of the innovation, when returns are feasible, there is improved access to private equity and public funding facilitating accommodation of different risk profiles through blended capital model involving loans, equity, grants, and even donations.

Homage was primarily funded by the founders' savings and grants in the early stages of research and prototype development. Recognising the social value, both public and private grants funded the iterations after the launch. Post-commercialisation, when proof of benefit and market opportunity was established, the potential for private capital funding strengthened. The founders reached out to angel investors to gain some buffer to fortify the innovation value before seeking return-driven private capital.

Homing in on growth: changing lives and winning accolades

Homage empowered and uplifted women in Singapore by offering them the convenience of managing their work around their family commitments and an opportunity to earn a regular income by trading their time, expertise, and service on their terms. The families of the seniors found some respite from the stressful chores of caregiving, while the seniors benefited from the reliable service offered at the comfort of their homes. The anecdotal accounts of financially empowered women and seniors with improved quality of care fuelled Homage's commitment to its mission. It won several accolades—Singapore's prime minister mentioned Homage as an upcoming start-up developing a socially relevant innovation in the National Day Rally 2017, and it won the 'Social Enterprise Start-Up of the Year' award at the President's Challenge Social Enterprise Award 2017.

Social innovations and systemic change

Social innovations targeting unmet social needs are capable of transforming society by effecting change to its systems (e.g., healthcare, education, and housing) through their wide-spanning outcomes. In essence, social innovations aim to change how social needs are conceptualised and how they are fulfilled.

A Schwab Foundation report uses the definition of Martin Fisher, co-founder and chief executive of Kickstart International, for systemic change, "Systems change is fundamentally, and on a large scale, changing the way a majority of relevant players solve a big social challenge, such that a critical mass of people affected by that problem substantially benefit."[8]

Every social innovation has systemic change as its goal, even if it does not achieve scale. Adoption and diffusion of innovation are fundamental to effect a systemic change. Even innovations that attain scale often fail in effecting systemic change because they lack organisational capacity to influence, convene, convince, advocate for, and counsel the intermediaries and actors in the system. To reach scale and fundamentally change the way things are done, social innovations require the complex interaction of cultural, legislative, political, and market elements. Depending on the context, factors influencing social innovations could act as drivers as well as barriers for diffusion and adoption of innovation.[9]

Hitting a home run

With the funding received, Homage began fortifying the app further and enhancing the marketing of its services. Homage was geared for growth, customer acquisition, and online visibility. Their hard work appeared to have paid off—in less than two years of rolling out the first version of the mobile app, the company was gearing up for growth. The founders had to find the means of driving up app subscription and use while bracing for the challenges involved in scaling the innovation.

Homage's potential to scale

The factors that determine Homage's potential to scale and effect systemic changes as a social innovation (SI) are primarily in favour of Homage. The innovation environment is conducive. There are service inadequacies resulting from the ageing population, declining support ratio, and increasing stress on public infrastructure and finance. The strict immigration laws in Singapore are presently a driver of the innovation that activates the latent workforce but would become a barrier when the adoption grows on the demand side but not on the supply side. The non-interventionist market-oriented governance and easy access to a mix of funding instruments are in favour of Homage.

The Homage app addresses the needs of the end users by providing flexible work and regular income to Care Pros and reliable and affordable home care for the Care Owners by mobilising the dormant workforce and easing the stress on the stakeholders, namely government and long-term care institutions. Regarding the leadership, the founders are willing to take risks, even to the extent of betting their careers and personal funds. In terms of technology, Singapore is well advanced, with one of the highest Internet and smartphone penetrations in the world.

Factors driving innovation adoption are mostly in favour of Homage. The solution is a likely alternative for the expensive conventional long-term care options available in the market. However, non-financial resources such as the physical and cognitive inabilities of the care recipients may act as a barrier for them to become direct users of the innovation. Institutional intermediaries will promote the innovation, and the prime minister's mention of Homage in his national address is a significant milestone besides the other awards that endorse the innovation. Increasing visibility will drive further adoption.

Social enterprise v. social innovation

Based on the definitions of the European Union,[10] Stanford Social Innovation Review,[11] and International Handbook on Social Innovation,[12] the key features of social innovation are:

- Novelty. Though not original, the SI must be new in terms of the application context or end users or must provide an improved value proposition compared to existing solutions.

- Creates new social relationships and collaborations.
- Benefits society as a whole and not just the actual beneficiaries or the local communities.

Though there is no consensus on the definition of social enterprise (SE), the following are identified as key features based on the definitions of Mohammad Yunus[13] and OECD:[14]

- They are conventional businesses trading goods or services.
- They have a social purpose.
- Their objective is not to maximise private wealth and profits.
- Profits are reinvested for achieving a social purpose.

SEs and SIs are related (refer to Table 7.1). While the former is a change agent, the latter is an execution mechanism. SEs harness the power of innovations to accomplish their social mission, and SIs need enterprises, especially SEs, to drive adoption and achieve scale.

Homage is organised as a profit-driven private entity, which distinguishes it from a social enterprise that typically functions as a non-profit or a hybrid. As a technology-based innovator, it is a cash-intensive innovation, so it makes sense to position itself as a profit-seeking private entity.

Table 7.1 Comparison of Social Enterprise and Social Innovation

Social Enterprise	*Social Innovation*
It is typically associated with the third sector.	It transcends sectors.
Has a well-defined social purpose to its mission.	May or may not have started with social purpose, but the value that it creates demonstrates social purpose. For example, the cab booking app Uber, improving mobility, resource sharing, income opportunities, and reducing environmental and transportation cost.
The impact is localised; beneficiaries are limited—a community or section of society. Even without scaling, it is still a SE.	Impact effects social change through widespread adoption and diffusion, resulting in policy reforms, behavioural changes, the institutionalisation of the model, and so on. Unless such systemic change happens, it will not be regarded as SI.

It also has a social purpose and the potential to radically change the caregiving landscape for the aged. Hence, Homage's innovation without the enterprise will not be able to effect systemic change. Likewise, the enterprise without the innovation, despite having a social purpose, would fail. Thus, the social innovation and the social enterprise are mutually reinforcing.

Scaling strategies

The means of achieving scale largely depends on what aspect of the impact/innovation the innovators want to scale.[15]

- *Dissemination:* Impact is scaled by spreading awareness through campaigns, advocacy, knowledge sharing, training, consulting, and lobbying. As awareness and recognition grow, independent organisations try to emulate the practices in other markets and communities. While this is the least resource-intensive and simplest strategy, founders have little or no control over mechanisms or entities replicating the model.
- *Affiliation:* Impact is scaled through synergistic affiliations with independent entities or licensees to replicate the model, and control can be exercised through formal agreements. More beneficiaries can benefit from replication. However, the failure of affiliates could affect the parent.
- *Direct Expansion:* Revenue growth is achieved through new products/service offerings or expanding into a new market. Direct expansion is resource intensive but translates to more beneficiaries and increased adoption and use cases.

Homage has to become financially sustainable by increasing the number of beneficiaries. Expanding into new geographies that have similar ageing issues through affiliations or direct expansion is not a feasible option because Homage has yet to prove its financial viability. Moreover, factors such as language, culture, and the regulatory and technological landscape could impede receptivity in new geographies.

Homage has to focus locally and drive adoption and usage by increasing subscription. However, a disproportionate increase of Care Pros and Care Owners would result in service latency, leading to attrition. So determining the optimum Care Owner to Care Pro ratio through data analytics is essential to ensure optimum incomes to the supply side and seamless service to the demand side of the value chain. Integrating a marketplace promoting products and services targeted at seniors and offering coupons and discounts for subscribers is another potential means to increase usage and subscription besides selling advertising spots.

Notes

1 Angelique Chan, Truls Ostbye, Rahul Malhotra, and Athel J. Hu, *Survey of Informal Caregiving*, Ministry of Social and Family Development, www.msf.gov.sg/publications/Pages/The-Survey-on-Informal-Caregiving.aspx.

2 Joanna Seow, "More Foreign Nurses Hired to Provide Home Care", *The Straits Times*, 11 June 2015, www.straitstimes.com/singapore/more-foreign-nurses-hired-to-provide-home-care.

3 Ministry of Health, "Health Manpower", www.moh.gov.sg/content/moh_web/home/statistics/Health_Facts_Singapore/Health_Manpower.html

4 "Fact Sheet, Enhanced Return-to-Nursing Training Scheme", Agency for Integrated Care, 11 August 2016, https://partners.aic.sg/sites/aicassets/AssetGallery/Factsheets/Factsheet%20-%20Return%20To%20Nursing_FINALAug2016.pdf.

5 Social Innovation Overview: A Deliverable of the Project, *The Theoretical, Empirical and Policy Foundations for Building Social Innovation in Europe (TEPSIE)*, European Commission – 7th Framework Programme, Brussels: European Commission, DG Research, Young Foundation, 31 May 2012, https://youngfoundation.org/wp-content/uploads/2012/12/TEPSIE.D1.1.Report.DefiningSocialInnovation.Part-1-defining-social-innovation.pdf.

6 Jeremy Millard and Gwendolyn Carpenter, "Digital Technology in Social Innovation, the Theoretical, Empirical and Policy Foundations for Building Social Innovation in Europe (TEPSIE)", November 2014, http://www.transitsocialinnovation.eu/content/original/Book%20covers/Local%20PDFs/124%20TEPSIE%20synopsis%20digital%20technology%20in%20SI.pdf.

7 "The Role of Private Equity in Social and Sustainable Development", *The Young Foundation*, March 2008, https://youngfoundation.org/wp-content/uploads/2013/02/The-Role-of-Private-Equity-in-Social-and-Sustainable-Development-March-2008.pdf; Rachel Keeler, "The Promise of Private Sector Grants in Impact Investing World", *Stanford Social*

Innovation Review, 29 November 2017, https://ssir.org/articles/entry/the_promise_of_private_sector_grants_in_an_impact_investing_world.

8 Hilde Schwab and Katherine Milligan, *Beyond Organisational Scale: How Social Entrepreneurs Create Systems Change*, World Economic Forum, May 2017, http://www3.weforum.org/docs/WEF_Schwab_Foundation_Systems_Report_2017.pdf.

9 Victor Bekkers, Lars Tummers, Bobby Glenn Stuijfzand, and William Voorberg, *Social Innovation in the Public Sector: An Integrative Framework, Learning from Innovation in Public Sector Environments (LIPSE Project)*, Working Paper Series No. 1; Katharine Schulmann and Kai Leichsenring, "A Qualitative Inventory of the Key Drivers of Social Innovation in Social Support and Long-Term Care, Mobilising the Potential of Active Ageing in Singapore (MOPACT)", December 2015, https://mopact.group.shef.ac.uk/wp-content/uploads/2013/10/D8.3-A-qualitative-inventory-of-the-key-drivers.pdf.

10 "Empowering People Driving Change: Social Innovations in the European Union", Bureau of European Policy Advisers. Publication Office of the European Union, France, 2011. p.9.

11 James Phills Jr., Kriss Deiglmeier, and Dale Miller, *Rediscovering Social Innovation*, Stanford Social Innovation Review, 2008, www.researchgate.net/publication/242511521_Rediscovering_Social_Innovation, accessed September 2018.

12 Frank Moulaert, Diana MacCallum, Abid Mehmood, and Abdelillah Hamdouch, eds., *The International Handbook on Social Innovation: Collective Action, Social Learning and Transdisciplinary Research*, Cheltenham: Edward Elgar Publishing, 2013, p.16.

13 Muhammad Yunus, *Creating A World Without Poverty: Social Business and the Future of Capitalism*, Philadelphia: Public Affairs, 2008.

14 Organisation for Economic Co-Operation and Development, *Social Enterprises*, France: OECD Publications, 1999, p.10.

15 Madeleine Gabriel, "Making It Big Strategies for Scaling Social Innovations", July 2014, (PDF file), www.nesta.org.uk/sites/default/files/making_it_big-web.pdf.

8

JUNTOS GLOBAL: DEPLOYING HUMAN-CENTRED DESIGN TO MOTIVATE THE NEWLY BANKED

Howard Thomas and Lipika Bhattacharya

Juntos Global (Juntos) specialises in deploying SMS-based solutions powered by data analytics capabilities for financial service providers to help them serve their newly banked customers more efficiently. The Juntos platform helps newly banked customers build formal savings habits through behavioural science strategies and principles of human-centred design (HCD) and builds a relationship of 'trust' between financial service providers and their customers.

Juntos uses an all-inclusive monthly subscription pricing mechanism based on the number of active users. An ethnographic study is conducted to design customised solutions for partner clients and agile practices are used for solution implementation. However, a long sales cycle of partnered projects and the need for scale to show measurable success act as major impediments to the firm's growth. Moreover, user behaviour is slow and tedious to change.

This case elaborates on the human behavioural issues related to financial exclusion and helps illustrate how behavioural economics and HCD can be used to enhance financial inclusion. It also highlights the inseparable link that exists between financial inclusion and social inclusion and the various dimensions of social inclusion that exist in the context of promoting financial inclusion for low-income communities.

The journey of Juntos had begun as a class project at Stanford's School of Design in 2010. Driven by the concept of design thinking, Ben Knelman,

DOI: 10.4324/9781003203582-9

then a student at the school, and his teammates had designed a tool to help janitors in the school build saving habits and feel more in control of their finances. By 2012, Juntos had garnered several global awards for its innovative solution. By 2017, the firm had implemented partnered projects in more than 15 countries and serviced more than one million users worldwide. The idea behind the Juntos solution was to motivate the poor to use formal financial services. The mechanics of the solution was derived from behavioural economics concepts like 'nudge' and 'elephant and rider.'[1]

When Knelman had started Juntos, he had built the solution with a social context in mind. The Juntos-automated SMS solution platform, Juntos Finanzas, was built with the objective of inculcating savings habits among the low-income newly banked customers of financial organisations. The aim was to keep such customers motivated towards using financial services regularly. The simplicity of design was a key consideration, and human-centred design formed the backbone of the solution. The platform built two-way communication with customers by basing the number and content of messages on customer reactions and was designed to be scalable with dynamic intelligence that could support millions of individualised, automated conversations simultaneously in multiple languages anywhere in the world. The platform was quickly deployable and could run parallel to a bank's IT system, minimising the need for lengthy integration cycles. A typical text message conversation between a customer and Juntos began with an introduction by the partner bank to their new SMS guide. Juntos then directly approached the customer with a reminder to use the service and asked further questions to help the customer.

Human-centred design

Through its interactions with newly banked customers, Juntos had realised that while obvious macroeconomic reasons like unemployment, poverty, and corruption limited financial access, mundane reasons like a vehicle with a flat tire or a dead cell phone battery could also be in the way of people using their accounts regularly. The Juntos platform had built-in automation to tackle such simple obstacles. Its SMS messages were designed to encourage saving habits in users by encouraging them to put away small amounts regularly. The platform tried to build habits slowly by providing information and lessening the emotional risks involved by engaging in real-time conversations with customers. From the bank's perspective, the relationship with low-balance customers also presented an interesting paradox. To be able to break even for such basic savings accounts, banks needed to increase the transactions and balances of customers significantly.

The Juntos business model was a partnership model, where the partner financial service provider was equally involved in the implementation of the solution, especially in the beginning of the project. For monetisation, the firm used an all-inclusive monthly subscription pricing mechanism based on the number of active users. At the start of every project, Juntos would conduct an ethnographic study to understand the target end customer. This helped uncover key behavioural and language traits, as well as insights into how trust could be built with the customers within that specific language and culture. A human-centred approach to the research helped in identifying user habits, needs, hopes, concerns, goals, and obstacles to the use of the products (such as a bank account or a mobile money account). Potential behavioural triggers that could influence increased usage were also identified. The findings from the ethnographic research were incorporated into the initial design, keeping in mind the interests of both the customer and the financial institution. The design was then pilot tested, with multiple conversation strategies evaluated simultaneously. The initial messages were designed for the pilot test by recruiting a small group of randomly selected individuals and tested to identify errors and misunderstood traits. Methodologies like A/B testing, rapid prototyping, and data science principles were used to fine-tune the messages and produce measurable financial behaviour change in the targeted customers. In terms of data analytics, the platform used qualitative data from user replies, as well as quantitative data on the number of people reacting to a particular message.

Following the implementation of the solution, results were analysed on a weekly basis to identify new insights, which were then incorporated into new conversations to be tested. For example, in their first deployment for a bank in Columbia, the staff at Juntos tried to maximise each message close to 160 characters when they started drafting the conversations. The objective was to provide users with comprehensive information to help them operate their mobile bank accounts. However, after watching a video of one of their users perusing his message aloud, they were surprised. It took the user more than 20 seconds to read the message in a halting and slow fashion. Such feedback helped the Juntos design team rethink the phrasing of their messages around user needs, who were often not conversant with either banking or mobile phones and had limited reading skills.

The iterative design process enabled Juntos to identify multiple successful conversation strategies and create a set of 'core' conversations that could potentially increase user engagement. The centralised processing of all data from a single platform helped detect lapses in data and generate timely alerts. The complete product lifecycle from design to copyediting, engineering, operations, and data analysis was executed through a single internal application. This enabled the testing of dozens of product variants within a span of a few weeks. The system also adapted its frequency of sending messages to the user's behaviour, sending multiple messages if the customer was highly engaged or fewer messages if the customer was not as responsive.

Performance reports from customer activity data were produced every two months for partner financial institutions. Insights gained from the reports helped identify strategies that were working. As the pilot projects were scaled, the platform also tracked and reported progress on the key performance indicators (KPIs) determined at the beginning of the project and the incremental impact of its solutions,

In some countries, Juntos was required by regulatory authorities to seek formal approval from customers to engage them on its platform. For example, regulations in Mexico and Columbia required customers to approve terms and conditions for using the service, while in some countries, customers could opt to receive certain types of content only.

Methodologies for behaviour change

Through interactions with the newly banked customers, Juntos had realised that myriad everyday difficulties could get in the way of people using their accounts regularly. Hence, building good communication with users to understand the manifold challenges they faced on a daily basis, and providing them with requisite advice, was essential to build savings habits and increase financial product usage. The key to building good communication with customers was to keep the SMS messages simple and build conversations (refer to Figure 8.1).

The messages sent from the platform were crafted based on HCD principles, with inputs from behavioural economics research. They were further refined with prototype trials to construct a dialogue that created strong relationships to drive higher account usage. HCD learnings were synthesised

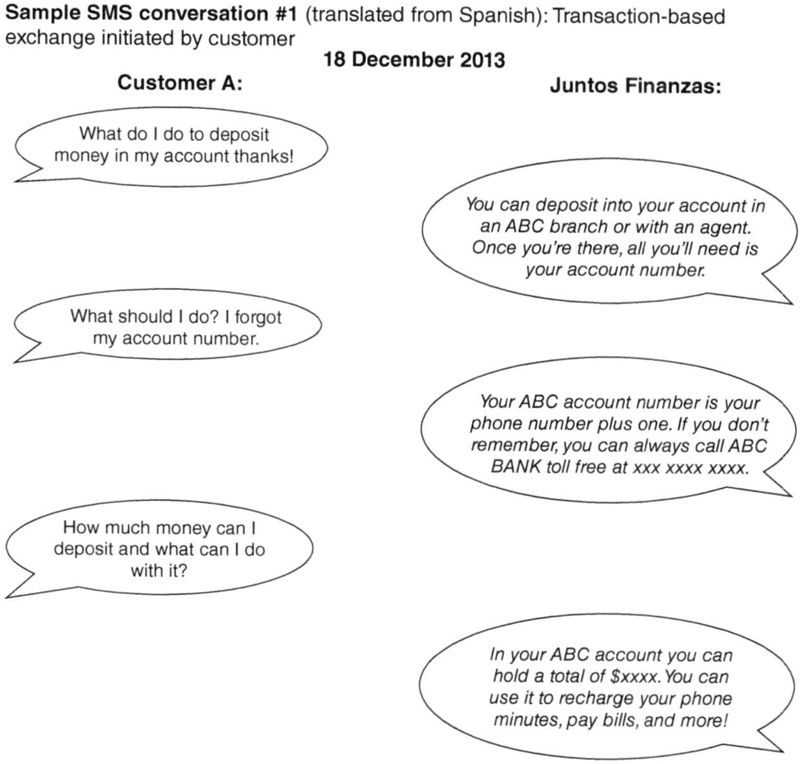

Figure 8.1 Juntos' SMS Conversation with User
Source: Company data.

from ethnographic interviews to identify user habits, needs, hopes, concerns, goals, and obstacles to the use of the products. Potential behavioural triggers that could influence increased usage were also identified. These learnings were then incorporated into the design to build appropriate messaging conversations for randomised control trials during the pilot phase. The ethnographic research was distinct in that it was meant to attain a deep understanding of a small subset of customers for inspiring product development. Both quantitative and qualitative data were used to drive product iterations. Financial transaction data, coupled with qualitative learnings from SMS conversations with users, was used to develop and revise the content further.

The iterative process of development had a much broader impact, as customer interaction with their financial services providers could be tracked, and insights from such messages could be used to improve the design of the messages. Moreover, the iterative design changes of the solution allowed the Juntos design team to understand user preferences and customise the solution to incorporate any unanticipated scenarios. Since each cycle got more feedback from customers on the efficacy of the solution, the solution was refined continuously. Juntos also conducted in-house research and incorporated findings produced by other behavioural researchers around the world into the design of its platform (refer to Table 8.1).

Table 8.1 Research Insights Used by Juntos

Research Insight	*Juntos Application*
Nudge by Richard Thaler and Cass Sunstein: By framing choices in a way that takes into account human biases, people can be "nudged" to better decisions.	Juntos never interacted directly with its user's money. Instead, it nudged its users to reach their savings goals through personalised text messages written with behaviour change principles in mind.
Switch by Chip Heath and Dan Heath: The human brain is divided, like an elephant and a rider. The elephant responds to emotion, while the rider responds to reason. When they disagree, the elephant wins. Changing behaviour (switch) requires directing the rider and motivating the elephant so that they move in the same direction.	Juntos directed the rider by asking users to pick a specific savings goal and motivated the elephant by encouraging users to keep within sight a photo that reminded them of their goal.
The Power of Habit by Charles Duhigg: There is a simple loop at the core of every habit consisting of three parts: cue, routine, and reward.	Empowering users to form savings habits began with cues in the form of text messages. These messages were sent regularly, helping to establish a routine. The most powerful reward that users received was not the money saved itself but rather the sense of confidence and control that they felt in their financial journeys.
Predictably Irrational by Dan Ariely: Not only do human beings make certain decisions that are irrational, we consistently and predictably do so. Even when we know we need to spend less and save more, we repeatedly don't stick to self-imposed budgets.	Because the technology enabled two-way conversations, it helped users feel that they were not alone in their financial journey. Juntos products helped users stick to their plans not only by providing an external source of accountability but also by providing an external source of validation.

Source: Company data.

While traditional economic theory assumed that people were rational, empirical evidence suggested that in addition to rationality as a motivating factor, people also exhibited emotions in their decision-making—these emotions were often referred to as cognitive biases. Hence, risk aversion would be a cognitive bias against risk and was likely to be stronger for people at the bottom of the pyramid (BoP). Wealthier people could take more risks, as their basic needs were taken care of, while poor people needed to ensure their survival. A behavioural research project conducted for a low-income population had noted that the savings goals of their clients were distant and abstract, while immediate financial needs and temptations felt pressing. Moreover, clients opened new savings accounts with little intention or plan about how to use the account to reach their savings goals.[2]

Economist Thaler had suggested that actions of people could be influenced or 'nudged' by slightly disturbing the environment or context of decision-making. These 'nudges' had the potential to overcome some cognitive biases and make people more open to considering solutions offered by businesses.[3] Juntos had applied behavioural insights and concepts like 'nudge' into a data analytics-driven solution to drive decision-making and changes in consumer behaviour. An important pre-requisite of using 'nudge' on customers was effective data collection of customer pain points and data monitoring. Collecting the data of the customers' usage of financial services and finding why customers stopped using some services was critical, as it helped identify customer pain points before a nudge could be applied.

Forging ahead

Juntos continuously incorporated the learnings from its implementations in its platform. For example, in its pilot test for a project with Tigo, Tanzania, Juntos had made several key observations. It had noted that the most popular SMS received from customers of Tigo were requests for shopping tips. The observations helped Juntos explore how its messages could offer key intelligence to better segment the customer base. Such analysis also helped partner financial organisations make intelligent decisions and optimise their strategies for targeting specific merchant categories or offerings of merchant products and discounts.

The services provided by Juntos acted as a trust-creating mechanisms to change the savings behaviour of the poor. However, user behaviour was often slow and tedious to change, and the biggest challenge for Juntos was to ensure faster change in user behaviour. The firm had explored various ways in which it could potentially further improve user behaviour by incorporating behaviour insights. One simple way to do this was to use the EAST (Easy, Attractive, Social, Timely) framework developed by Insights (2014).[4] To implement EAST, Juntos could potentially deploy the following strategies (refer to Figure 8.2).

1 Make It Easy: In its current practice, Juntos would ask its customers if they would like to opt in and only then allow them to use its solution. To improve the usage of its solution, Juntos could let customers have access to the solution by default. Juntos could then ask customers why they had moved away from the default option, if they chose to do so. In such a scenario, more people would be likely to use the solution, even if they were initially not interested in the service.
2 Make It Attractive: Through learning analysis from its projects, Juntos had realised that people chose SMS options that were presented attractively. Another way of achieving attractiveness was to add images, colour, and personalisation to messages. At the same time, keeping messages short

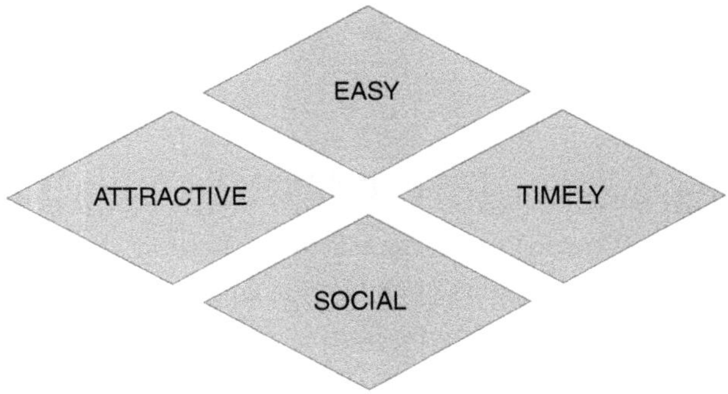

Figure 8.2 Implementing Behavioural Change with the EAST Model

Source: EAST: Four Simple Ways to Apply Behavioural Insights, The Behavioural Insights Team, www.behaviouralinsights.co.uk/publications/east-four-simple-ways-to-apply-behavioural-insights/.

and simple was also essential, especially since most users of the services were likely to be less educated.

3 Make It Social: The tendency of herd behaviour was well documented in behavioural economics; hence, giving examples of peoples' choices encouraged others to follow the same decision. One way this could be achieved in the Juntos platform was to build messages quoting how many people from the community were already using its services, thus encouraging users to follow the trend. Moreover, the option of continuing with the financial service could be presented to customers in appealing colours with images of the financial institution and data about other customers in the community who had similar demographic and social backgrounds and were already using the service.

4 Make It Timely: It had also been observed that people were most likely to change their behaviours at specific times; for example, they were more likely to spend money on items when they received their paychecks. If the savings messages could be sent on the first of the month, which was the payday for most people, the need to save could be recognised to a greater extent.

Another challenge Juntos faced in its project implementations was the lack of understanding of how to handle SMS messages. A key reason for this hurdle was illiteracy. An SMS-based solution required a minimal level of literacy, which the poor in certain geographies lacked. Given the various challenges, could the Juntos solution be modified for the illiterate poor?

While the Juntos platform was primarily SMS driven, going forward, as voice technologies got cheaper and readily available in mobile phones, customers could potentially speak into their devices for receiving help. Towards this end, could voice technologies be the next possible step in the evolution of the Juntos platform?

Notes

1 Richard H. Thaler and Cass R. Sunstein, *Nudge: Improving Decisions about Health, Wealth, and Happiness*, Turabian, 2009, https://www.researchgate.net/file.PostFileLoader.html?id=53abe564cf57d7df1e8b45f4&assetKey=AS%3A273548994646025%40 1442230571326.

2 Centre for Applied Data Analytics, "Visualisation & Analytic Interfaces, Changing User Behaviour: Nudge Along", www.ceadar.ie/pages/changing-user-behaviour-nudge-along/.
3 Ibid.
4 The Behavioural Insights Team, EAST: Four Simple Ways to Apply Behavioural Insights, www.behaviouralinsights.co.uk/publications/east-four-simple-ways-to-apply-behavioural-insights/.

9

BETTR BARISTA: A SHOT AT BETTER LIVES

Heli Wang, Sheetal Mittal, and Adeline Natalia Lai Sue Yi

In this case study, Pamela Chng, the founder of Singapore-based Bettr Barista, believes that a workplace cannot exist aloof from society's challenges and that companies need to be accountable for their contribution to society. Bettr Barista is her attempt to go beyond the pure profit motive and improve the lives of marginalised women and youth in the city-state. The enterprise offers a four-month-long holistic programme, equipping them with job skills as a barista. Bettr Barista's large menu of for-profit businesses, including internationally certified speciality coffee education and training workshops, a coffee roastery, retail coffee outlets, and mobile brew bars, supports and sustains its social mission.

The case highlights the challenge in maintaining the balance between financial and social goals, as this drives most of the decisions taken by the company, be it its value chain or the key stakeholders. The social role on one hand may accord the company a differentiated position in a fragmented and congested industry; on the other hand, it adversely affects the company's productivity and resources utilisation and hence its ability to grow.

In 2011, Pamela Chng launched Bettr Barista (BB) as a coffee academy that offered disadvantaged women and youth in Singapore a four-month-long holistic programme providing barista skills for employability, emotional and

DOI: 10.4324/9781003203582-10

physical training skills for psychological wellbeing, and an internship for learning on the job. At the end of the programme, BB helped the trainees secure employment in the industry. By the end of 2018, it had trained and placed more than 60 individuals with the support of government bodies, social-sector organisations, and private-sector companies.

To support and sustain its social goals, BB undertook for-profit coffee workshops for corporates and individuals and ran other commercial businesses, including a coffee roastery, retail coffee outlets, and mobile brew bars. By the end of 2018, the coffee company had served 397,000 cups of coffee to 212,000 consumers through its cafés and mobile bars and held more than 430 corporate events.

However, in order to be truly sustainable, Chng realised that BB needed to expand internationally, as the Singapore market was small and offered limited growth potential. Many of the neighbouring countries, being primarily coffee-drinking markets, were attractive options. However, this also raised many concerns, as such a strategy could stretch the company's already limited financial and managerial resources. BB's business model was unique to Singapore, and the level of market development, technology, governance structures, and government support varied significantly across countries in the region. Would BB have the expertise and resources to change or tweak its approach according to each country's market dynamics? Additionally, executing expansion plans would require a comprehensive management structure to be put in place at BB. Could all of this be done without affecting the core values the company stood for?

The invisible poor in Singapore

Singapore was hailed as one of the world's richest countries. However, while the living conditions among Singapore's poorest were not as dire as in other countries in the region, about 14 percent of its citizens faced severe financial constraints and could not afford even their basic requirements.[1] Over 2012–2015, there was an increase of about 43 percent in the number of families living in poverty and dependent on government assistance, the worst result to be reported officially in Singapore.[2] In 2015, the country had one of the largest inequality gaps in advanced Asian countries.

As of June 2016, after the elderly (60-plus years), Singaporeans between 15 and 34 years of age were the most financially affected group, with around

5 percent unemployed (double the other age groups) and about 41,500 working in low-paying entry-level jobs earning below S$1,000 a month. The adverse financial condition of the young workers could be attributed to three key factors: they were born into poverty, they were stuck in low-paying jobs, or they were unemployed.

According to Chng, people with challenging backgrounds often struggled in Singapore's highly competitive education system. She explained, "If you fall behind, you stay behind. It is very difficult to catch up."

Bettr Barista

Why a social enterprise?

As the founder of a web consultancy business, Chng found herself burnt out in the fast-paced and intensely competitive digital domain and decided to quit in 2009. At that time, she became interested in establishing a socially responsible venture. She explained,

> *We all spend more than half of our life in a workplace; thus, a workplace cannot exist aloof from society's challenges. Companies need to be accountable for their contribution to society by creating work places and businesses that make peoples' lives better. I wanted to create a new business that went beyond pure profit motive.*

Chng rejected the donation-based NGO model for its lack of sustainability and lack of independence in operations. She also believed that charity was good for developmental work where it was not possible to make profits and hence envisioned a self-sustaining financial model that had the potential to create market-generated resources.

Setting up the business

Chng was joined by Jeanette Lee and Randall Lee as partners, and together they invested over US$158,000 as seed money for the venture. Analysis of the industry led them to understand that the revenue stream from the coffee education business would not be adequate to achieve financial viability, and hence multiple revenue streams had to be created by developing competencies in the areas of roasting and retailing.

In November 2011, BB was launched as a coffee academy, followed soon by its roastery, retail café outlets, and mobile espresso brew bars. To minimise the capital expense, Chng acquired the distributorship of Astoria roasting and brewing coffee equipment from Italy, enabling the start-up to get not only ready access to the equipment but also affordable prices. Next, Chng rented an 800-square-foot space to set up the academy and company's head office.

Coffee academy

At the academy, BB ran two programmes in the professional coffee education space: a regular one for full-paying customers and a social one that was highly subsidised.

Regular programme

The regular programme offered professional courses of varying lengths, from a day to a week, across a range of functions along the coffee supply chain, such as barista, roasting, or sensory training. The courses were globally recognised, with international certification by the Specialty Coffee Association of America (SCAA) and Specialty Coffee Association of Europe (SCAE), and were meant for people who wanted to make a career in the coffee industry or for those who had a passion for coffee and wanted to learn more about it.

Using her digital domain expertise, Chng developed the website for the company and activated social media platforms to create awareness, engage with the target audience, and drive enrolment. At the end of the first year, BB had trained about 150 candidates—a number that grew to 4,300 candidates from over 30 countries by the end of 2018. Entrepreneurs, especially from countries such as Indonesia, Vietnam, the Philippines, and Malaysia, came to learn about the coffee business to set up cafés in their home countries. In 2018, the regular programme contributed 35 percent of BB's total revenue.

Social programme

The social programme was a comprehensive training course for the marginalised section of the society, especially youth and women. It was developed based on the insights Chng drew from her interactions with a number of social service organisations in Singapore. She explained,

> *I learned that providing the skills training was not an issue, the problem was that they would not get jobs after training, and if some of them did, they could not retain the job for long. This was not because of lack of skills, but because their emotional and psychological issues were not addressed.*

BB's holistic social programme aimed at ensuring the trainees' physical and emotional wellbeing, besides providing them barista and roasting skills. The objective was to help them acquire a sense of self-worth and dignity, become fully job ready, and be economically independent. The programme, originally conducted over six months and subsequently reduced to four months, comprised one month of intensive study, followed by one month of internship and two months of on-the-job training.

The focus in the first month was on both coffee education and emotional training. The content for the latter, developed in conjunction with a clinical therapist, was based on the Rational Emotive Behaviour Therapy model that helped people build emotional resilience. It affected all aspects of their life—health, work, family, and social. The physical training component, which included yoga, trekking, mountain climbing, self-defence, rock climbing, and canoe rowing, was conducted on the weekends of the first two months. Supported by Singapore's Ministry of Social and Family Development (MSF) through a grant from ComCare Enterprise Fund,[3] BB was able to heavily subsidise the cost of the programme (US$2590) and charged the trainees only US$222.

In addition, the programme was adapted per the needs of a particular target segment. For example, BB provided training to the inmates at juvenile detention centres and Changi women's prison (some of whom continued with the programme even after being released). BB also used the coffee education platform to engage young students from challenging neighbourhoods who had a high risk of dropping out of school.

By 2018, BB was working with more than 80 social service organisations that not only referred potential beneficiaries to the programme but also helped deal with the personal issues of those selected. At the end of first year, four trainees (out of a total intake of seven) graduated. However, with time, the retention rate improved considerably.

In the early years, when BB did not have any of its own outlets, internships and employment were only possible with other retail cafes. Once BB started opening its own retail outlets, it could employ many of its own trainees, and that environment was much better suited in retaining and developing them. Chng explained,

> *BB has developed a massive support system and our people are trained to deal with the issues of marginalised people so that they do not slip through the cracks along the way. But in the commercial world, nobody builds and devotes the bandwidth to be that forgiving and kind. If you do not show up for work, you are fired, as pure business set-ups have a lot of pressure to stay afloat. Although this makes being competitive in the marketplace twice as hard for us.*

In 2018, of BB's total workforce of 50 (including part-timers and contract staff), 40 percent were graduates from its own social programme, who worked across the enterprise's different business units. Its social programme had enrolled 100 candidates by early 2018, of which 70 percent graduated successfully. Of these, 90 percent were employed, with only a 10 percent dropout rate as of the end of 2018.

Other businesses

Coffee roastery

Focused on keeping its entire supply chain green, the roastery carefully selected the suppliers from whom it sourced coffee beans. It worked directly with farms and B-Corps,[4] who were accredited as having treated their farmers and employees fairly and ethically. More than 50 percent of the roastery's output was used by BB's academy and coffee bars, ensuring a continued green chain across its businesses. In 2018, the coffee roasting unit contributed 15 percent of BB's total revenue.

Mobile brew bars

In mobile bars, the temporary coffee bars set up for an event or occasion, the most important resource was a 'trained barista.' With BB having a ready access to them, it had an advantage over others in being able to set up large number of bars even at short notice. By the end of 2018, the business unit contributed 15 percent of BB's total revenue, having set up more than 400 mobile bars and served over 200,000 cups of coffee.

Retail coffee outlets

By the end of 2018, BB had four public outlets and four outlets inside corporate offices, with plans to open many more over the next couple of years. Together they generated 35 percent of BB's total sales.

Corporate partners

Since 2013, DBS Bank had been engaging BB for setting up mobile brew bars to serve coffee at their corporate events. In 2014, when the DBS Foundation was set up, the bank decided to collaborate with BB to help create financial sustainability in the community. It awarded BB with a scale-up grant and in 2017 sponsored BB's outlet in the bank's lobby at Plaza Singapura, a shopping mall located along the main shopping street of the city-state. Additionally, BB was given preferential transaction rates with no required minimum monthly balance for DBS banking services. Similarly, BB's relationship with NTUC Income, an insurance cooperative, had initially started as a commercial one. Soon after, NTUC Income's Orange Aid foundation provided the company start-up funding for setting up its first few retail locations.

Integrated management approach

BB practised an integrated approach to policy formulation and management across its business units. All the strategic decisions related to finance, operations, human resources, vendor selection, or purchasing were taken while keeping in mind their impact on society, environment, and other industries and ensuring traceability of its supply chain. Furthermore, while there were dedicated teams for each business unit, most employees had dual responsibilities. Irrespective of their core roles, all were cross-trained across businesses and functions.

BB had a truly diverse workforce. On one hand, it comprised school dropouts, ex-convicts and former drug addicts, and on the other, it included people with PhDs and international work experience. While this made BB a challenging place to work for new recruits, it also led to a rich culture born out of the intermingling of varied experiences, knowledge, and skill sets.

Trade-off

The dichotomy between the financial goals and social goals required a constant balancing act. For example, BB's workforce included many of its own graduates from the social programme, who required a more compassionate approach, as their productivity and efficiency levels at the beginning tended to be lower. This compromise was inevitable, despite being a significant cost to business. In addition, whenever the social programme was held, most of the training and infrastructure resources were committed to it, limiting BB's capacity to undertake commercial activities, thus adversely affecting the revenue and profitability of the company.

To some extent, the previous conflict was resolved in mid-2017 when BB invested in a new space for its head office and academy, which was three times the size of the earlier one, opening up the possibility of undertaking simultaneous workshops.

Growth and sustainability

In 2013, BB won the President's Challenge Social Enterprise Start-up of the Year award, followed by Social Enterprise of the Year award in 2017. In 2015, it became the first and only certified B-Corp in Singapore—one of the 2,600 companies recognised as B-Corp across more than 150 industries and 60 countries. In addition, in 2015, BB hit profitability with its revenue growing at 40–50 percent (year-on-year). The continued rapid growth over 2015–2017 prompted BB to invest the profits accrued, in addition to a loan, in creating bigger infrastructure, hiring more manpower, and opening more retail outlets in Singapore.

Going forward, in the case of its social goals, BB's focus was to deliver a high-quality programme with long-term impact, and thus it aimed to keep the intake low. Chng explained,

> *Given the background of the trainees, it was important to provide each trainee adequate one-to-one support and, that was possible only if we limited the total number of intakes to a maximum of four every year with not more than 10 to 12 trainees each time.*

On the other hand, regarding its commercial ventures, BB was keen to scale up its operations in order to become a self-sustaining social enterprise that was not dependent on subsidies and grants.

However, given that Singapore was a small market, Chng knew that it would be difficult to continue to grow at the same pace as in the recent past. The focus within the country would have to be increasingly towards stabilising the team and operations, targeting bigger clients, and generating recurring revenues, whereas for growth, BB would have to look beyond Singapore. Would that mean stretching itself too thin by growing too fast, both financially and structurally?

Another concern was the lack of a middle layer of managers and leaders in the organisation. Chng knew that for BB to grow into its next phase successfully, it was imperative to develop an effective management structure. Chng mused, how could BB maintain the social element at the core of everything it did yet continue to stay relevant and sustainable in the long term?

Resource-based view and evaluation of BB

The resource-based view (RBV) evaluates the potential of an organisation's resources in creating sustainable competitive advantage through the lens of four attributes, known as the VRIO framework (refer to Table 9.1).[5]

Contribution to creating value

A company uses its resources to create value for its customers. The value created must distinguish the company's offering from that of the competition; only then does the resource(s) qualify to be valuable. The key valuable resources of BB are:

- Industry Expertise: Chng invested heavily in acquiring competence in the coffee domain. Her understanding of the industry led her to acquire the distributorship of an Italian coffee equipment manufacturer and identify the appropriate suppliers for sourcing coffee beans that ensured a green value chain. She also recognised that the coffee industry was conducive to imparting vocational skills to people even if they lacked formal education.

Table 9.1 Evaluation of BB's Key Resources

Key Resources	*Contribution to Creating Value*	*Rarity*	*Inimitability*
Technical expertise—product and industry	Acquisition of superior-quality coffee ingredients and coffee-making equipment; development of a green value chain	Medium	Can be imitated, but at a cost
Market knowledge	Identification of the market gap in coffee education and skills training—high demand for trained baristas; ineffectiveness of only-technical training programmes	High	Can be imitated
Unique training programme	Comprehensive training across all dimensions: technical, physical, and psychological, enabled financial and social inclusion of disadvantaged individuals	High	Difficult to imitate
Vertically integrated supply chain	Manages a high degree of control over the supply, quality, and delivery of ingredients and finished products; pro-environment approach; mobilisation and optimal utilisation of resources such as manpower and capital assets; high operational efficiency and lower costs	High	Can be imitated, but at a high cost
Brand equity	Brand image as socially responsible	High	Difficult to imitate
Digital marketing	High awareness and enrolment	Low	Can be imitated

- Market Knowledge: Knowledge of the consumption trends led Chng to identify the widening gap between the supply and demand of suitably qualified manpower to service the mushrooming speciality cafés in the country.
- Holistic Training Programme: In-depth research into the existing vocational training programmes that had been ineffective in addressing

the needs of disadvantaged individuals helped BB to identify what elements in a training programme are critical for success. This led BB to collaborate with a clinical therapist and develop a comprehensive module that helped people build emotional resilience. The training programme thus designed focused on all aspects of an individual's life—health, work, family, and social.

- Integrated Supply Chain: Another key capability of BB is its vertically integrated value chain model. The strategic approach has enabled the company to not only financially support its primary goal of creating social impact but also deliver on high operational efficiency; control over quality and costs; leveraging synergies across business units; optimisation of resources; and, most importantly, ensuring a pro-environment, fair, and fully traceable supply line.
- Brand: BB's branding, woven around its 'social contribution,' is the source of key differentiation in the highly competitive coffee market in Singapore. BB stands out from other speciality cafés on account of the social impact it creates and the green practices it has adopted.
- Digital Marketing: Chng's expertise in digital marketing (on account of her previous work experience) has provided BB a low-cost platform to reach its target market quickly and directly.

Rarity

Resources that are available to few are considered rare. If most players can acquire the same resource, then each of them has the same capability, leading to what is known as competitive parity. Only if a resource is both valuable and rare can a company create competitive differentiation. Some of BB's valuable resources, such as market knowledge, brand equity, an integrated supply chain, and holistic training programme, are rare as well, while others, like digital marketing and technical expertise, are easily available.

Inimitability

To build long-term competitive advantage, it is important that the resources of a firm, besides being valuable and rare, also be difficult/costly to copy or substitute. In the case of BB, it can be argued that while its market knowledge and integrated value chain can be acquired by competition (albeit at a cost), its training programme and brand equity are difficult to imitate or replace with an alternative.

Organisation

Incorporation of the social element in its training as well as brand image requires a passionate organisational culture to support it. BB, through its integrated management approach and commitment to its social mission, can be considered to have exploited its resources effectively to make social objectives an integral and indispensable part of its business. Moreover, unlike the rest of the industry, BB's retail business is not stymied by the lack of availability of qualified manpower, as it has access to the trained candidates its academy churns out regularly. Similarly, its brand image of being socially responsible has enabled the company to collaborate with a number of partners across the public, private, and social sectors.

BB's social strategy enabled the company a new way of achieving differentiation and sustainability in an otherwise highly competitive market. While it is possible for other companies to replicate this business model, it will be effective only if there is an integral change in their vision and mission. Using the social positioning just as external packaging is a short-term tactical approach which can be imitated easily by me-too players and hence will not help create a sustainable competitive advantage in the industry.

Going forward, in order to increase the scale of its social impact, BB needs to generate higher income from its for-profit operations. Paradoxically, it is the conflict between BB's commercial and social programmes that adversely impacts its financial performance. While international expansion seems attractive, it requires significant investments.

Notes

1 States Times Review, "Ministry: Poverty in Singapore Reached Worst Ever, Jumped 43.45 Percent in 3 Years", 22 April 2017, http://statestimesreview.com/2017/04/22/ministry-poverty-in-singapore-reached-worst-ever-jumped-43–45-in-3-years/.

2 Ibid.

3 The ComCare Enterprise Fund (CEF) is instituted by the Ministry of Social and Family Development with an objective to provide funding to social enterprise start-ups.

4 Certified B Corporations (B-Corps) were businesses that met the highest standards of verified social and environmental performance, public transparency, and legal accountability to balance profit and purpose. For more information, refer to https://bcorporation.net/about-b-corps.

5 Jay Barney, "Firm Resources and Sustained Competitive Advantage", *Journal of Management*, 17(1) (1991): 99–120, www.business.illinois.edu/josephm/BA545_Fall percent202019/Barney percent20(1991).pdf.

10

BASE OF PYRAMID HUB: CONNECTING SOLUTIONS

Jonathan Chang and Lipika Bhattacharya

Jack Sim established Base of Pyramid Hub in Singapore with the objective of providing professional services to social entrepreneurs to develop and scale solutions for the BoP market. The BoP represents 2.7 billion people across the world living in poverty. Serving this market segment has social as well as economic incentives. Sim notes that the "poor need all kinds of things—like clothing, food, water filters, cooking stoves, vehicles, entertainment products, solar lamps, low cost housing, sanitation, education, healthcare, pharmaceuticals etc. Social enterprises can come together to provide cost effective solutions that target these needs." However, the key challenge faced by social entrepreneurs is the issue of 'financial sustainability.'

BoP Hub had established a 'market based model' to help social entrepreneurs scale their initiatives. However, lack of traditional fundraising methods, a common organisational strategy, and a well-understood model for scaling continued to act as impediments. Moreover, short programme timelines, very stringent accountability requirements by the sources of available funding, and high expectations of showing results were significant bottlenecks for social entrepreneurships. Could a refined business model address these challenges and bring unprecedented efficiency for entrepreneurs like Sim in the BoP market?

It was October 2016, and Jack Sim, founder of Singapore's Base of Pyramid Hub (BoP Hub) had just finished speaking to the media about his vision for

DOI: 10.4324/9781003203582-11

the enterprise. Sim came up with the idea of the BoP Hub in 2011, at a time when the poor appeared to have easier access to mobile phones than to clean drinking water. The world's population had been growing at an alarming rate over the past few decades, and more than 60 percent of it lived in poverty—a demographic that was also known as the base of the pyramid (BoP).[1]

A significant portion of the BoP lived in Asia. However, with Asian economies improving rapidly, a ubiquitous observation was that people who were currently in the BoP would soon become the middle class as they gained better access to education and economic development. This gradual shift in wealth indicated the value of developing a BoP market. It also created the potential for developing new markets, driving economies and creating more jobs in the process.

BoP Hub was established with the aim of providing professional services to social entrepreneurs catering to the BoP market and helping them develop and scale their businesses through the BoP Hub platform. The primary objective of the platform was to allow social enterprises in Singapore and South Asia to share knowledge and create workable designs to serve the BoP population. The vision was to engage the poor as entrepreneurs, workers, and sales representatives by providing them with adequate training. Additionally, the objective was to act like an accelerator to replicate and bring to scale best practices, proven business models, and technologies such that all stakeholders—investors, social entrepreneurs, corporations, academia, technology pioneers, local community leaders, and government agencies—could collaborate to align their missions and work in synergy to create maximum impact.

Challenges of the BoP market

Sim had noted that designing solutions specifically for the BoP market had some known challenges. While in Western economies, the extremely poor were often supported by government schemes, in developing economies, they were largely left to their own means to meet their basic needs. Some people in the BoP segment earned fixed monthly incomes, while other were daily wage earners. This created a unique demand set that was subject to varied income and expenditure levels, due to which product or service solutions could rarely be interchangeable or readily transferable even within the segment across various markets.

Another drawback was that the primarily rural base of the BoP communities was often located in remote areas and subject to harsh climatic conditions, making it challenging to design solutions specific to their needs. The rural base of the target population also implied slow dissemination of knowledge to end customers, since they had little exposure to existing customer experiences from outside their local communities. Low literacy levels were another inhibiting factor that ruled out marketing and communication materials commonly used by most commercial companies. Poorly executed and intermittent government schemes had resulted in the acceptance of low-quality products that challenged the end customer's perception of better product choices. Additionally, short-term subsidy programmes led to skewed price point perceptions.

Moreover, lack of civic and private infrastructure in rural markets, such as roads, water channels, electricity, and telecommunications, created an entry barrier for affordable, mainstream products. It also added an additional financial burden on manufacturers to distribute their products efficiently, as they had to be designed in such a way that their operations and maintenance were more suited to local infrastructure availability and long-term market-based solutions.

Another significant problem faced was the "poverty penalty," where the poor actually paid more for amenities like drinking water, healthcare, food, and utility items. This was primarily because the BoP market was not well developed, and there was not enough competition to bring down prices. The price point was also lower, as affordability was much less. The poor brought very small packets of food and utility items, as their meagre income allowed them to purchase items only on a day-to-day basis, usually in cash. For these reasons, big corporations often found it hard and expensive to enter this market. An example was the Pur water purification powder manufactured by Procter & Gamble, which failed to generate a competitive return in the BoP market despite its low pricing and product relevance.[2] Sim felt that because of its unique structure, the BoP market could only be served by small-scale social enterprises.

Market-based model

While providing the poor with access to technology and necessities could help them improve their quality of life over the short term, for a long-term solution, the poor had to become self sufficient.[3] This meant not only providing them with access to basic amenities and resources but also helping them earn the means to afford these resources. Hence, there was a need for a market-based model that could provide product solutions and create employment (refer to Figure 10.1).

Observing the relevance of the market-specific products for the BoP segment, Sim had launched the Sanishop project in 2014. The micro franchise programme trained local entrepreneurs to build toilets (onsite sanitation systems) that were then sold to the poor at an affordable price of US$45. The Sanishop programme was established successfully in Cambodia, India, Vietnam, and South Africa. The project built toilets for more than 11,000 households in Cambodia. It also trained over 500 sales entrepreneurs within the community across seven provinces in the country.

Another successful project that Sim initiated was the World Toilet College, in partnership with the Global Interfaith WASH Alliance, a religious group in India wherein local entrepreneurs sold toilets on a commission basis. Such income generation not only helped the rural poor in gaining employment but also provided good sanitation facilities to the people, promoting safer and healthier lifestyles.

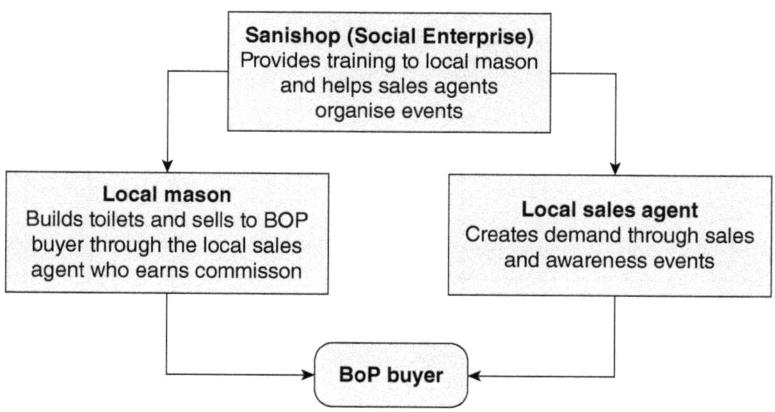

Figure 10.1 Market-Based Model for BoP

Source: WTO, what-we-do, "Sanishop Social Franchisee Model", http://worldtoilet.org/what-we-do/sanishop/.

Sim had also launched the 45Rice initiative, which served to improve the nutrition of meals consumed by 350,000 low-income construction workers in Singapore. Noticing that the workers' meals consisted primarily of 700 grams of white rice accompanied by small portions of chicken curry and vegetables, he had partnered with DSM, a Dutch pharmaceutical company, to substitute white rice with rice fortified with vitamins in the meals.

The funding dilemma

Sim had noted that the major impediment to the growth of social entrepreneurships was their inability to attract significant funding for long-term sustenance. He had tried to assess various financial instruments to obtain funding for social entrepreneurships (refer to Table 10.1).[4]

One such financial instrument was loan guarantees. The advantage of opting for a loan guarantee over grants was the efficiency of leveraging limited funds while enjoying the same amount of payment certainty as a grant. Many organisations had used loan guarantees to spearhead their projects. One example was that of the Bill & Melinda Gates Foundation, which had provided a charter school in Houston a loan guarantee to raise US$67 million in commercial debt at a low rate, saving the school (and its donors) almost US$10 million in interest payments.

Quasi-equity debt was another option preferred for financing projects for the BoP. For such loans, interest could be indexed to the financial performance of the social enterprise. Such an instrument could therefore give the investor a return that would be similar to that of a structured equity.

Social entrepreneurs could also attract funding purely on the premise of high return on investment (ROI). Just like conventional entrepreneurs, the

Table 10.1 Debt and Quasi-Debt Instruments of Financing Available to BoP Hub

Type	*Convertible Debt*	*Debt*	*Securitised Debt*
Payment structure	Fixed with conversion	Fixed	Fixed
Claim on assets	Preferred	First	Off balance sheet
Type of return	Medium risk and return	Low financial risk and return	Tailored to investor types

Source: Bugg-Levine, Kogut & Kulatilaka, "A New Approach to Funding Social Enterprises", Harvard Business Review, January 2012, pp. 123.

BoP Hub and its clients could potentially use their business plans and concepts to attract different kinds of funding based on the risk-return portfolio, that is, equity funding, bonds, loans, and so on. One of the avenues available to the BoP Hub and its clients who generated small returns was to have a mix of charitable investments from donors and then promise a higher return to investors. They could thus have a mix of funding sources looking for social returns and financial returns. While the social donor could be willing to invest money for social returns, the investor would be looking for financial returns. By unbundling the social returns and the benefit of the investment for different investors, the BoP Hub could increase the scale of return offered to potential investors.

Social entrepreneurs could also request charitable donations from larger firms that were serving the target market. For instance, a fundraising project for the rehabilitation and reconciliation of the victims of the Irish War in the 1960s had sought charitable donations from the general Irish diaspora and rich Irish citizens in the United States. Their efforts were very successful, as the Irish-origin community in the United States felt strongly about helping the victims of the war.[5] Such initiatives illustrated that seeking funds from individuals or groups who shared a common ethnicity or other bond with the community being helped was more likely to be successful.

Another very important source of funding for the BoP Hub and the social entrepreneurs it served was crowdfunding. Some crowdfunding sites like Fundly.com, Kickstarter.com, StartSomeGood.com, Indiegogo.com, and Rockethub.com[6] actively supported social entrepreneurs. On many crowdfunding sites, donors made charitable contributions and did not expect financial returns. Enterprises like BoP Hub could approach crowdfunding donors either for matching funds or for giving better returns to investors on equity and debt instruments.

Scaling

For the BoP Hub, scaling was essential to reach more social entrepreneurs and expand the suite of support services available to them on the platform. BoP Hub could scale up by having larger revenues and more clients and serving more geographies. There were several options available for it to scale across geographies. Sim, however, had mixed feelings about how he could further refine the business model to scale up his initiative with maximum impact.

He could use professional service providers to recommend his platform to social entrepreneurs and run multiple projects of similar scope across several countries. Alternatively, he could use the platform for knowledge services and pilot projects in one location (for example, Singapore) and then use its experience to expand to other countries in Southeast Asia. Another plausible approach for BoP Hub was to take advantage of its core strengths as an organisation and adopt the 'beanstalk' configuration, where the momentum for system change could come from the founder.

Social enterprises like BoP Hub had to ensure a supply of raw materials and labour when scaling into different geographies. Researchers had often discussed ensuring supply when scaling, and why it was critical to a firm's growth.[7] Social enterprises designing products or services for the BoP also created market connections with export markets when information about the export markets was generated by formal-sector organisations. The formal-sector organisations then shared this information with BoP producers.[8]

Growing concerns

While funding projects for the BoP were the primary issue that bothered Sim and his team on an ongoing basis, there were other concerns as well. With a small team operating out of Singapore and supported by volunteers, BoP Hub operated like most other non-profit organisations, striving to execute projects efficiently with limited resources and funding. For Sim, the primary challenges in advancing the platform to catalyse innovative products and services for the BoP included lack of access to traditional fundraising methods, the need of a common strategy for entrepreneurs serving the BoP (leading to multiple services being required by them), and the requirement of a well-understood model for scaling the businesses.

In 2016, despite having several options for funding, Sim was at crossroads. How could he build more collaborations and attract investment and support groups to help expand his firm's outreach? Summing up the scalability needs of BoP Hub, Sim concluded, "We need to design a comprehensive fundraising strategy and effective organisation structure to scale our BoP Hub initiative. So how do we do that?"

Notes

1 World Bank, "Poverty Definition", http://data.worldbank.org/topic/poverty.
2 Erik Simanis, "Reality Check at the Bottom of the Pyramid", *Harvard Business Review*, 2012, https://hbr.org/2012/06/reality-check-at-thebottom-of-the-pyramid.
3 Encyclopaedia Britannica, "Bottom of the Pyramid", https://global.britannica.com/topic/Bottom-of-the-Pyramid.
4 Antony Bugg-Levine, Bruce Kogut, and Nalin Kulatilaka, "A New Approach to Funding Social Enterprises", *Harvard Business Review*, January 2012, p. 123.
5 Edna McGovern, "An International Social-Marketing Strategy for a Non-Profit Organization: Determining the Path for Continued Success", *Journal of Case Studies*, 30(1) (June 2012): 27–43.
6 Devin Thorpe, "Eight Crowdfunding Sites for Social Entrepreneurs", *Forbes*, 10 September 2012, www.forbes.com/sites/devinthorpe/2012/09/10/eight-crowdfunding-sites-for-social-entrepreneurs/#438baea870fa.
7 Anne Parmigiani and Miguel Rivera-Santos, "Sourcing for the Base of the Pyramid: Constructing Supply Chains to Address Voids in Subsistence Markets", *Journal of Operations Management*, 33–34 (January 2015): 60–70.
8 Souleïmane Adekambi, Paul Ingenbleek, and Hans van Trijp, "Integrating Producers at the Base of the Pyramid with Global Markets: A Market Learning Approach", *Journal of International Marketing*, 23 (December 2015): 44–23.

CONCLUSION

Sheetal Mittal

Reflections

Through the different case studies discussed, this book highlights the different models that social enterprises can adopt and pursue effectively. However, one of the key learnings that shines through all these cases is the role of social capital in driving social inclusion and financial empowerment of disadvantaged groups in a society. Social capital can be defined as the ability of people to work together for common purposes in groups, their willingness to live by the norms of one's community and to punish those who do not.[1] Thus, building social capital, and hence a supportive social network, is a fundamental step for a social enterprise to gain the acceptance and trust of not only the target segment and their families but also the community at large. And this has come through across nations—be it Vietnam, as in the case of iCare; Philippines's Great Women; India's Veriown; Bangladesh's SureCash; or Myanmar's Fullerton Holdings and Yangon Bakehouse. The case studies also demonstrate that women social entrepreneurs in particular are very effective in developing and enabling such networks.

In 1983, the founding father of social entrepreneurship, Professor Muhammad Yunus, used the social capital mechanism to establish Grameen Bank in Bangladesh.[2] Recognising the inability of the target market to provide collateral and pay high interest rates, he created social networks of five

DOI: 10.4324/9781003203582-12

to ten members from the local community, which an individual must join to be eligible for loans. The loans are issued on the principles of mutual trust, relationship, accountability, and participation of the community, and each member shares the responsibility for the loans granted to any member of the group. By 2019, Grameen Bank had disbursed collateral-free loans of US$24 billion to more than 9 million borrowers, opened 2,568 branches across 81,678 villages, and covered more than 97 percent of the total villages in Bangladesh.[3]

In fact, one of the most effective strategies is to identify the social ecosystems and use the social capital within them to drive the shared goal. Increasingly viewed as a critical asset for individuals and households at the bottom of the pyramid, in the early 2000s, leading social organisations such as the World Bank and Ashoka Foundation decided to focus on the role of social capital in delivering community welfare and alleviating poverty and its difference from other resources such as physical and human capital. However, close to two decades later, research in the domain still falls short of fully understanding how social capital is developed, deployed, and managed by social enterprises in underdeveloped resource-constrained regions and communities.[4]

Another critical element for any social enterprise model is its ability to create social value effectively. The case studies highlight how these social entities strive to provide their target markets access to the supportive inputs necessary for driving inclusive growth and raising productivity. While these inputs may vary based on a region's extent of development (or the lack of it), they can be broadly classified as: basic inputs such as electricity, water, transportation, health, education, and infrastructure networks; enabling inputs that enhance productivity such as financial services networks, logistic systems, and legal and property rights; and complementary inputs such as professional and training networks, knowledge, and social networks.[5] Take the example of Bettr Barista in Singapore and Yangon Bakehouse in Myanmar: two similar business models but with widely different economies and cultures, particularly in relation to their state of development, legal acceptance of the concept of a social enterprise, and involvement of government agencies in the social sector. Despite these differences in context, both organisations cater to marginalised groups that are devoid of similar basic inputs—physical and psychological wellbeing, education, rights awareness, and vocational skills for employability.

Social enterprises such as iCare, Fullerton, SureCash, and Juntos provide their target markets with enabling inputs, such as access to financial service networks, to help them become more productive and participate actively and consistently in the labour force. Veriown strives to offer both basic and higher-level inputs by providing access to energy, the Internet, and financial services. However, lack of a complementary input—a social network—hinders its ability to access last-mile consumers. On the other hand, enterprises such as Homage and BoP Hub have used technology to overcome value chain constraints. They have created social, professional, and training networks that provide their target individuals and groups the opportunities to collaborate, access skills and knowhow, and use and render services.

It is important to appreciate that a social enterprise creates both economic and social value as it works for the betterment of the society by supporting it through its for-profit operations. The challenge is maintaining the balance between these two goals, as often an enterprise finds itself at a crossroads when its limited resources can support either its social mission or financial goals. The dilemma is evaluating what it should focus more on in situations of conflict of interest. If it prioritises revenues, it is no different from a 'for-profit' business. On the other hand, if it uses its resources for its social mission at the cost of productivity and profitability, it may not continue to be financially sustainable. Thus, a social enterprise must ensure that the value added at each touch point corresponds to the organisation's dual mission and is not overly inclined towards one, since both play a pivotal role while complementing each other. The social role accords the enterprise a differentiated position in the industry and thus a competitive advantage in the market. This enables it to be a preferred partner among stakeholders and generate economic value, which in turn is used to sustain and grow the social impact.

The solution probably lies in understanding that a social enterprise's return on investment comprises a mix of social impact and financial revenues. It is wrong to assess its performance and the ability to raise funds only in terms of economic returns it generates. As Bugg-Levine, Kogut, and Kulatilaka (2012) suggest, a social enterprise needs to adopt hybrid financial instruments that bundle risks and returns in different proportions, as sought by different types of investors. Even charitable donations that offer no financial return may be an attractive investment opportunity for those who seek only social impact.

In summary, it is important to understand the differences in vision, strategy, resources, and business model of a social enterprise *vis-à-vis* a purely for-profit venture or NGO. For a social enterprise to sustain or scale up its operations, it must (1) practice a bottom-up social capital-based approach, (2) ensure efficiencies in its whole value chain and create and capture value at each touch point, and (3) adopt innovative financial restructuring and enter into social impact partnerships.

Acknowledgements

The founding team—the "Pioneers" of Singapore Management University (SMU)—instilled the tradition of community service and social responsibility in the institute's DNA right at the beginning. This deeply held commitment has been sustained and enriched over the years by its faculty members, research assistants, and students across its schools and centres, such as the Lien Centre of Social Innovation and Centre of Social Responsibility. SMU also houses one of Asia's leading, multiple award-winning case centres, the Centre for Management Practice, that has added to the momentum behind the social research and development agenda by engaging with social entrepreneurs, writing up their stories, and sharing them in the form of case studies with the world at large. We strongly believe that the motivations, tribulations, successes, and even failures of these social entrepreneurs are critical for continued learning, contribution, and innovation in the domain. The writing of this book has been very much part of this journey.

In this endeavour to propagate and stimulate inclusive growth, MasterCard has been a valuable and indispensable partner. The MasterCard Foundation, established in 2006, joined hands with SMU to fund a Social and Financial Inclusion Research Program from 2015 to 2018, with a geographical focus on ASEAN. The partnership successfully undertook a number of research projects, widened and honed the domain expertise, and built on the existing knowledge by promoting the development of most of these case studies.

We would like to believe that the journey has only commenced, and there is much yet to be done in showcasing and learning from the stories of these social entrepreneurships.

Notes

1 Dewan Mahboob Hossain, "Social Capital and Microfinance: The Case of Grameen Bank, Bangladesh", *Middle East Journal of Business*, October 2013, www.academia.edu/4645508/Social_Capital_and_Microfinance_The_Case_of_Grameen_Bank_Bangladesh.

2 Muhammad Yunus, *Building Social Business: The New Kind of Capitalism That Serves Humanity's Most Pressing Needs*, New York: PublicAffairs, 2010.

3 Grameen Bank, "Data and Report", www.grameen.com/monthly-report-2020-05-issue-485-in-usd/#.

4 Howard Thomas and Yuwa Hedrick-Wong, *Inclusive Growth: The Global Challenges of Social Inequality and Financial Inclusion*, Bingley, UK: Emerald Group Publishing, 2019.

5 Ibid.

INDEX

Page numbers in *italics* indicate a figure and page numbers in **bold** indicate a table on the corresponding page.

For Product Safety Concerns and Information please contact our EU representative GPSR@taylorandfrancis.com
Taylor & Francis Verlag GmbH, Kaufingerstraße 24, 80331 München, Germany

www.ingramcontent.com/pod-product-compliance
Ingram Content Group UK Ltd.
Pitfield, Milton Keynes, MK11 3LW, UK
UKHW020001200926
475702UK00015B/2411
9781032067315